Ten years ago Pamela Westland left London and her job as editor of a women's monthly magazine to live in the country with her husband, Douglas, and five cats and 'just write books'. Her first cookery book, *A Taste of the Country*, was a wistful look at what she had been missing – the joy of cooking with all the home-grown fruit, vegetables and herbs a small town garden couldn't provide. Gradually what began as nostalgia has grown into a campaign, and all her cookery books have a message – to use the best possible natural ingredients, cooked in the most convenient way. 'Save time by using modern appliances by all means,' she says, 'but don't squander your family's health by using processed-out foods.'

Her two most recent books illustrate this point perfectly. In *The Complete Grill Cookbook* she shows how contact grills and sandwich makers can produce 'real food' that anyone would be proud of – and indeed, Pamela used only those appliances during the time she was writing the book – and that included Christmas! And in *High-Fibre Vegetarian Cookery* she pioneers for the health awareness that her grandmother, a professional cook, quite naturally took for granted.

By the same author

PAMELA WESTLAND

High-Fibre Vegetarian Cookery

GRANADA
London Toronto Sydney New York

Published by Granada Publishing Limited in 1983

ISBN 0 586 05905 9

A Granada Paperback Original
Copyright © Pamela Westland 1983
The fibre and calorie factors in the Dietary Fibre Chart on
page 266 are taken from *The Composition of Foods* by McCance
& Widdowson, 4th ed. revised by Paul & Southgate,
reproduced by kind permission of Her Majesty's Stationery
Office.

Granada Publishing Limited
Frogmore, St Albans, Herts AL2 2NF
and
36 Golden Square, London W1R 4AH
515 Madison Avenue, New York, NY 10022, USA
117 York Street, Sydney, NSW 2000, Australia
60 International Blvd, Rexdale, Ontario, R9W 6J2, Canada
61 Beach Road, Auckland, New Zealand

Printed and bound in Great Britain by
Collins, Glasgow.
Set in Baskerville

Contents

Introduction

Vegetarians are off to a very good start, since dietary fibre – the substance now convincingly shown to be important in the prevention of many common Western diseases and ailments – is present only in plants. It forms the cell wall and rigid structure of plant foods of all kinds – nuts, seeds, berries, cereal grains, pulses and other fruits and vegetables – the very foundation, of course, of a vegetarian programme.

Research has shown that we in the Western world consume something between only one-third and one-sixth of the dietary fibre taken by peoples in under-developed countries – in parts of the world, that is to say, where food is not processed to give it a finer texture, a whiter colour or greater rising capacity. And it is Western peoples, having allowed even their staple foods such as wheat to be tampered with in this way, who are prone to coronary heart disease, cancer of the large bowel, diverticular disease of the colon, appendicitis, gall-stones, diabetes, haemorrhoids, varicose veins and obesity.

Because dietary fibre contains no nutriments it was until recently largely discounted as an important part of a healthy diet – although one brand of all-bran breakfast cereal has for generations been regularly prescribed by anxious parents as a cure for constipation. Now it is widely recognized that by increasing the volume and softness of the bowel content – and thereby speeding up its journey through the gut; and by affecting the metabolism and absorption properties of substances present in the bowel, fibre does indeed have a vital role to play in the health of people of all ages.

It has been estimated that the average Western intake of fibre is as low as about 20 grams a day – the equivalent of, for example, five 50-g (2-oz) slices of wholewheat bread. Doctors researching the effect of dietary fibre in preventive medicine recommend that something like double that intake – at least 30–35 grams a day – would be a healthier goal to set ourselves.

This does not, of course, mean that we should eat eight or nine slices of bread a day – heaven forbid! – or that we need to sprinkle our foods with spoonfuls of chaffy bran – heaven forbid again.

To vegetarians, and to others of us who enjoy the delicious variety of plant foods, it is easy to achieve the recommended fibre intake with perhaps only a small change of emphasis in the things we eat. For fruits, vegetables and other plant foods vary in fibre content just as they do in calorific value.

Whole cereal grains are one of the most important and versatile sources of fibre. A glance at the fibre chart (page 266) shows the value, in fibre terms, of insisting on *wholewheat* bread and of using *wholewheat* flour for pastries and all other forms of baking. Brown rice and wholewheat pasta, with both their delicious nutty flavour and pleasantly chewy texture, contain significantly more fibre than polished 'refined' rice and 'refined' pasta, and are therefore strongly emphasized throughout the following chapters.

Among the vegetables, it is the legumes and dried pulses that have the most to offer in fibre terms, and so it is well worth including them in one of their different roles in at least one meal a day. Spinach is another 'goody' vegetable, with other leafy greens, mushrooms and some roots not far behind. Watery vegetables like courgettes, marrows and tomatoes are down near the bottom of the class, but there's no need to banish them entirely – recipes for courgettes filled with cauliflower and beans; tomatoes with spinach; green peppers with sweetcorn purée or prunes and hazelnuts; marrow packed with lentils – all give ideas for combining high- and low-fibre ingredients, and getting the best of both textures.

It's the same with fruits. Some of the most readily available and popular ones – oranges, apples, pears, peaches and strawberries, for example – are relatively low in fibre. When making fruit salads, the trick is to combine these with black or redcurrants, blackberries, raspberries or logan-berries which have a significantly higher fibre count, and to add nuts and dried fruits whenever possible.

All dried fruits are a fibre-counter's dream. Dried apricots contain 24 per cent, against 2.1 per cent in the fresh fruit; dried peaches 14.3 per cent against 1.4 per cent; and raisins 6.8 per cent fibre compared with a count of 0.9 per cent for fresh grapes. And so in the chapters on fruit salads and puddings – in other sections too – every trick in the trade is shamelessly employed, using dried fruit purée as a sauce, mixing fresh fruits with their dried counterparts, adding chopped dried fruits to baking mixtures, fillings for vege-tables and savoury salads.

Nuts and seeds can be clearly seen as important high-fibre additives, with almonds rating 14.3 per cent fibre content, peanuts 8.1 per cent and desiccated coconut 23.5 per cent. The possibilities are endless – chopped nuts in salads; toasted nuts adding crunch to macerated fruits; sunflower seeds to garnish soups; peanut sauce with steaming hot vegetables; sesame seeds and coconut crisping-up cookies – it's an exciting and tasty challenge.

A word on the sometimes confusing subject of peeling fruit and vegetables. (Manufacturers of potato and apple peelers, please accept my apologies.) As so much of the fibre is concentrated in or near the skin, I have a rule, 'scrub, not scrape', which I rarely break. Take apples – there's only 2.0

per cent fibre in the flesh, but 3.7 per cent in the peel. Enough said!

In a book which sets out to highlight the advantages of dietary fibre there is not space for a thesis on fats, or an extension of the complicated issue of saturated versus mono-unsaturated and polyunsaturated fats. Readers will no doubt have their own preferences and their reasons for them. The general rule of thumb I have used is this: I have specified butter and olive oil for dishes where I felt the flavour was particularly important, and oil or margarine in all the others. Naturally your own preferences will prevail and perhaps in many cases over-rule mine.

A vegetarian programme based on these recipes should provide not only the dietary fibre but also the nutrients the body needs. And because high-fibre foods are both filling and satisfying, it should be possible, by careful selection of the recipes, either to lose weight or effortlessly maintain a steady weight.

Before I started planning and testing recipes for this book, I was what a friend calls 'a two-day-a-week vegetarian'. After months of practising what I am preaching, so to speak, I have found myself more than ever delighted by the texture, the colour, the straight-from-the-garden flavour that typifies imaginative vegetarian cooking. I hope you will be too.

1 Soups

Soups are all excellent potential purveyors of dietary fibre. First of all, it's important to start with a good home-made, well-flavoured stock. Once you have that – following the first recipe in this chapter – you can make an endless variety of thick and creamy soups by cooking one or more types of dried, root or green vegetables in the stock and liquidizing them to a smooth purée packed with our hidden ingredient, all the original vegetable fibre.

Alternatively, you can simmer a medley of fresh vegetables, dried pulses or wholewheat pasta shapes in the stock and serve them crispy-tender, colourful and appetizing, floating in the still clear and by now highly flavoured liquid. As taste is such an individual thing, and preference varies, always sample a little of the soup before serving and make any last-minute adjustments. Apart from the obvious salt and pepper, a dash of lemon juice, mushroom ketchup and soy sauce, a pinch of sugar, curry powder or grated nutmeg can all work wonders.

If the stock or purée needs thickening, use wholewheat flour, wholewheat semolina or bran to achieve a rich, nutty flavour – and lots more fibre.

Garnishings are important both visually and in terms of food value. Fresh vegetables, either grated (e.g. carrots) or cut into decorative flower shapes (page 53), floating on a pale creamy soup become colourful highlights – and tasty ones, too. Build up a stock of ready-made 'bakery' garnishes to add interest and 'bite' to your soups. Croûtons (made with wholewheat bread of course), breadcrumbs, or crushed bran crispbread dry-fried with chopped onion, nuts or spice or flower seeds add enormously to a soup's personality. And the recipes are all here. When supplies run out, improvise with straight-from-the-tin garnishes of fennel or sunflower seeds, chopped or toasted nuts, dried fruits and even cocktail savouries.

For a more substantial meal-in-a-pot, you can make soups more nourishing by stirring in eggs to scramble or dropping them in whole to poach in a clear soup; by stirring grated or cubed cheese into the soup just before serving; or by beating in double cream, plain yoghurt or buttermilk to make 'cream-of' soups richer still.

And to serve with the soup? There's farmhouse-fresh wholewheat bread or rolls, of course; cheese, herb, nut or plain wholewheat soda bread or scones, cheese straws, or matchstick-thin vegetable strips such as carrot, parsnip, cucumber, celery and red or green peppers (page 52).

If you are following a low-fat diet, you might prefer to make a simple adjustment to many of the soup recipes and omit the initial fry-in-fat step, and go straight into the simmering stage. That way, you'll lose a little flavour and a lot of calories!

VEGETABLE STOCK

The better the stock, the better the soup. Use whatever vegetables you have, even trimmings and peelings, and have a supply of stock always on hand. If you wish to freeze the stock, you can reduce it by boiling until it is half the volume, then on thawing make it up by adding more water.

2 large onions, halved (not peeled)
2 large carrots, halved
6 stalks celery, halved

1 clove garlic, peeled and halved (optional)
a bunch of fresh herbs
4 bay leaves
about 1 kg (2¼ lb) chopped vegetables (or trimmings)
    such as potatoes, turnips, cabbage, cauliflower, Brussels
    sprouts, green beans, pea pods, leeks (do not use broad
    beans)
15 ml (1 tablespoon) black peppercorns, lightly crushed
10 ml (2 teaspoons) yeast extract

Put all the ingredients into a very large pan and add as
much water as it will take – say about 4 litres (7 pints). Cover
and bring slowly to the boil. Simmer for about 2½ hours. Set
aside to cool, then strain the stock when it is cold. Store in a
covered container in the refrigerator.

You can give the stock even more flavour by using
'vegetable water' to make it – always strain and save the
liquid in which you have boiled or steamed vegetables. A
word of warning – be sure any cooking liquid you add to
stock is not over-salty.

Makes about 2 litres (3½ pints)

BEETROOT SOUP

450 g (1 lb) small beetroots
25 g (1 oz) margarine
1 large onion, peeled and chopped
1 large carrot, chopped
2 medium potatoes, chopped
2.3 litres (4 pints) vegetable stock (page 12)
15 ml (1 tablespoon) red wine vinegar, or other vinegar
15 ml (1 tablespoon) tomato purée
salt and pepper

For serving
soured cream
sunflower seeds

Wash the beetroots and tear off all but about 7.5 cm (3 in) of the tops. Cook them in a covered pan of boiling water for 35–40 minutes, until they are just tender. Drain the beetroots, rub off the skins and cut off the tops. Cut the beetroots into matchstick strips and set aside.

Meanwhile, melt the margarine in a large pan and fry the onion over moderate heat for 4–5 minutes, stirring once or twice. Add the carrot and potatoes, stir well and pour on the stock. Cover the pan, bring to the boil and simmer for 20 minutes. Liquidize in a blender and return to the pan.

Stir in the vinegar and tomato purée, season with salt and pepper and add the beetroot strips. Simmer for 15 minutes. Taste and adjust the seasoning to your liking.

To serve, stir in soured cream, or float a little on each portion. Hand sunflower seeds separately.

Serves 8–10

CURRIED BEAN SOUP

A storecupboard stand-by makes a quick high-fibre soup.

    25 g (1 oz) margarine
    1 medium onion, peeled and chopped
    1 clove garlic, peeled and chopped
    450 g (1 lb) cooking apples, cored and chopped
    2 × 225-g (8-oz) cans curried baked beans
    600 ml (1 pint) water
    salt and pepper
    60 ml (4 tablespoons) sultanas
    1 dessert apple, cored and thinly sliced

Melt the margarine in a pan and fry the onion and garlic over moderate heat for 3 minutes, stirring once or twice. Add the chopped apples, stir well, then stir in one can of beans and the water. Bring to the boil, cover the pan and simmer for 20 minutes.

Liquidize the soup in a blender, return to the pan, add the second can of beans and season with salt and pepper. Heat gently. To serve, scatter the sultanas into the soup and float the apple slices on top.
Serves 6

LEEK AND PASTA SOUP

25 g (1 oz) margarine
1 medium onion, peeled and chopped
900 g (2 lb) leeks, well washed and sliced
1 large potato, chopped
1.4 litre (2½ pints) vegetable stock (page 12)
175 g (6 oz) wholewheat pasta wheels
salt and pepper
30 ml (2 tablespoons) chopped chives

Melt the margarine in a large pan and fry the onions and leeks over moderate heat for 5 minutes, stirring occasionally. Add the potato and the stock, cover the pan and bring to the boil. Simmer for 20 minutes.

Liquidize in a blender and return to the pan. Add the pasta, season with salt and pepper, cover the pan and bring to the boil. Simmer for 15 minutes, or until the pasta is just tender. Taste and adjust the seasoning if needed. Garnish with the chives.
Serves 6

PEANUT AND YOGHURT SOUP

25 g (1 oz) margarine
1 medium onion, peeled and sliced
1 medium carrot, chopped
100 g (4 oz) unsalted peanuts
700 ml (1¼ pints) vegetable stock (page 12)
75 ml (5 tablespoons) medium sherry (optional)

    salt and pepper
    150 ml (¼ pint) top of milk
    150 ml (¼ pint) natural yoghurt
    20 ml (4 teaspoons) peanut butter

    For garnish
    15 ml (1 tablespoon) chopped fresh parsley

Melt the margarine in a pan and fry the onion over
moderate heat, stirring occasionally, for about 3 minutes.
Add the carrot and cook for a further 2 minutes.

Rub the peanuts in a cloth to remove the brown skins, add
them to the pan and stir well. Pour on the stock, cover, bring
to the boil and simmer for about 40 minutes. Liquidize the
vegetables, peanuts and stock in a blender. Return the purée
to the rinsed pan, add the sherry if using, and season well
with salt and pepper.

In a basin, beat together the milk and yoghurt. Stir this
mixture into the soup and heat gently without boiling. Taste
and adjust the seasoning if needed. Just before serving, stir in
the peanut butter and garnish with the parsley.
Serves 4

PROVENÇAL SOUP

    25 g (1 oz) margarine
    1 medium onion, peeled and chopped
    2 stalks celery, thinly sliced
    2 cloves garlic, peeled and crushed
    2 medium carrots, thinly sliced
    1.7 litre (3 pints) vegetable stock (page 12)
    450 g (1 lb) French or runner beans, trimmed and sliced
    225 g (8 oz) courgettes, sliced
    100 g (4 oz) wholewheat pasta rings
    salt and pepper

For serving
croûtons (page 30)
grated Parmesan cheese (optional)

Melt the margarine in a large pan and fry the onion, celery
and garlic over moderate heat for 4–5 minutes, stirring once
or twice. Stir in the carrots, pour on the stock and cover the
pan. Bring to the boil and simmer for 15 minutes.

Add the beans, courgettes and pasta and season with salt
and pepper. Cover again and simmer for a further 15
minutes, or until the pasta is just tender. Taste and adjust
the seasoning if needed.

Serve the croûtons separately with Parmesan cheese and
plenty of warm wholemeal bread. The soup makes a
substantial meal.
Serves 6–8

VEGETABLE MEDLEY

25 g (1 oz) margarine
1 medium onion, peeled and sliced
1 clove garlic, peeled and chopped
1 leek, well washed and sliced
2 stalks celery, thinly sliced
1 medium carrot, cut into matchstick strips
1.4 litre (2½ pints) vegetable stock (page 12) or water
salt and pepper
30 ml (2 tablespoons) tomato purée
225 g (8 oz) firm white cabbage, shredded
75 g (3 oz) cooked dried beans (e.g. kidney, haricot)
50 g (2 oz) wholewheat macaroni, broken into small pieces

For serving
grated Parmesan cheese

Melt the margarine in a large pan and fry the onion, garlic, leek and celery over moderate heat for 4 minutes, stirring once or twice. Stir in the carrot and pour on the stock. Season with salt and pepper, cover and bring to the boil. Simmer for 10 minutes.

Stir in the tomato purée and add the cabbage. Simmer for another 5 minutes. Add the cooked beans and macaroni and simmer for a further 15 minutes, or until the pasta is just tender. Taste and adjust the seasoning if needed. Serve the Parmesan cheese separately.

Serves 6

OATMEAL SOUP WITH PARSLEY DUMPLINGS

25 g (1 oz) margarine
2 large onions, peeled and sliced
2 medium carrots, thinly sliced
1 small turnip, finely diced
1 leek, well washed and thinly sliced
50 g (2 oz) rolled porage oats
600 ml (1 pint) vegetable stock (page 12)
600 ml (1 pint) milk
salt and pepper
30 ml (2 tablespoons) chopped fresh parsley

For the dumplings (optional)
50 g (2 oz) self-raising wholewheat flour
a pinch of salt
25 g (1 oz) butter, grated
15 ml (1 tablespoon) chopped fresh parsley
5 ml (1 teaspoon) yeast extract
15 ml (1 tablespoon) warm water

Melt the margarine in a large pan, add the vegetables and fry over moderate heat for 4–5 minutes, stirring occasionally. Sprinkle in the oats and stir well. Cook for 2 minutes. Gradually pour on the stock, stirring all the time. Cover the pan, bring to the boil and simmer for 30 minutes.

Meanwhile make the dumplings. Mix together the flour, salt and butter and stir in the parsley. Dissolve the yeast extract in the water. Mix the dry ingredients with just enough of the liquid to make a firm dough, and shape into 12 small balls.

Pour the milk into the soup, season well with salt and pepper and stir in the parsley. Bring just to simmering point and add the dumplings. Simmer for 8-10 minutes, until the dumplings have risen to the top and are just firm. Do not allow the soup to boil. Adjust the seasoning if needed – the soup should be very well seasoned.
Serves 6

CELERIAC AND POTATO SOUP

450 g (1 lb) celeriac, scrubbed
30 ml (2 tablespoons) lemon juice
1 large onion, peeled and sliced
2 medium potatoes, peeled and chopped
1.1 litres (2 pints) vegetable stock (page 12)
1 bouquet garni
salt and pepper
60 ml (4 tablespoons) plain yoghurt

For the topping
50 g (2 oz) margarine
1 medium onion, peeled and finely chopped
120 ml (8 tablespoons) wholewheat breadcrumbs
45 ml (3 tablespoons) chopped walnuts
10 ml (2 teaspoons) celery seeds

Cut the celeriac into dice and immediately toss them in the lemon juice to preserve their colour. Tip them into a pan with the onion and potatoes, pour on the stock and add the bouquet garni. Bring slowly to the boil, cover and simmer for 30 minutes. Discard the bouquet garni and liquidize the soup in a blender. Season well with salt and pepper and stir in the yoghurt. Reheat gently.

To make the topping, melt the margarine in a pan and fry the onion over moderate heat for 2–3 minutes. Stir in the breadcrumbs and stir-fry for another 2–3 minutes, until the crumbs are dry and golden brown. Stir in the walnuts and celery seeds. Scatter the topping over the soup immediately prior to serving. Alternatively make quantities of the topping in advance; cool it completely and store in an airtight jar, ready for use.

Serves 6

* Substitute celery for the celeriac – but you might have to sieve away any extra-stringy pieces. Or ring the changes and use Jerusalem artichokes – fennel seed could then replace celery seed in the topping.

SWEETCORN AND WATERCRESS CHOWDER

    25 g (1 oz) margarine
    1 large onion, peeled and chopped
    2 medium carrots, diced
    1 green pepper, seeded and chopped
    350-g (12-oz) can sweetcorn kernels
    700 ml (1¼ pints) water
    5 ml (1 teaspoon) lemon juice
    salt and pepper
    150 ml (¼ pint) plain yoghurt
    ½ bunch watercress, finely chopped

    For serving
    parsley croûtons (page 31)

Melt the margarine in a pan and fry the onion over moderate heat for 2–3 minutes, add the carrots and pepper, stir well and cook for a further 2 minutes. Tip in the can of sweetcorn, add the water and lemon juice and season with salt and pepper. Cover, bring to the boil and simmer for 25-30 minutes.

Reserve about 30 ml (2 tablespoons) of the vegetables. Liquidize the remainder in a blender and return to the pan. Stir in the reserved vegetables and the yoghurt and adjust the seasoning. Heat gently without boiling. Stir in the watercress and serve. Hand the croûtons separately.

Serves 4

LENTIL AND ORANGE SOUP

30 ml (2 tablespoons) vegetable oil
1 large onion, peeled and sliced
2 medium carrots, chopped
2 stalks tender celery, thinly sliced
2 medium potatoes, chopped
175 g (6 oz) split red lentils, washed
1 litre (1¾ pints) vegetable stock (page 12)
1 orange, seeded and roughly chopped
salt and pepper
1 can frozen concentrated orange juice

For serving
4 medium carrots, diced and cooked
orange croûtons (page 31), optional

Heat the oil in a pan and fry the onion, carrots, celery and potatoes over moderate heat for 3 minutes. Stir in the lentils then pour on the stock, add the orange and season with salt and pepper. Cover, bring to the boil and simmer for about 1 hour. Liquidize the soup in a blender.

Return the soup to the pan, add the orange juice and heat slowly. Add more seasoning if needed. Stir in the cooked

carrot dice, for extra texture and colour, and allow them just to heat through. Serve the croûtons separately.
Serves 6

SPINACH SOUP

50 g (2 oz) margarine
1 medium onion, peeled and chopped
5 ml (1 teaspoon) ground coriander
350-g (12-oz) packet frozen leaf spinach, thawed
850 ml (½ pints) vegetable stock (page 12)
salt and pepper
10 ml (2 teaspoons) lemon juice
1 bay leaf
15 ml (1 tablespoon) wholewheat flour
60 ml (4 tablespoons) plain yoghurt

For the topping
25 g (1 oz) margarine
60 ml (4 tablespoons) wholewheat breadcrumbs
30 ml (2 tablespoons) sunflower seeds

Melt half the margarine in a pan and fry the onion over moderate heat for 2 minutes. Stir in the coriander and cook for a further 2 minutes. Add the spinach, stir well, then add the stock, salt, pepper, lemon juice and bay leaf. Cover the pan, bring to the boil and simmer for 20 minutes. Discard the bay leaf and liquidize the soup in a blender.

Melt the remaining margarine in the cleaned pan, stir in the flour, and when it has formed a roux, gradually pour on the purée, stirring all the time. Bring to the boil and simmer for 5 minutes. Stir in the yoghurt.

To make the topping, melt the margarine in a pan and fry the breadcrumbs, stirring frequently, for 3–4 minutes, until they are dry. Stir in the sunflower seeds and mix well.

Scatter this mixture on the soup at the point of serving, or serve separately.
Serves 4

KIDNEY BEAN CHILLI

50 g (2 oz) margarine
2 large onions, peeled and chopped
2 cloves garlic, peeled and chopped
4 stalks celery, thinly sliced
10 ml (2 teaspoons) chilli powder, or to taste
45 ml (2 tablespoons) tomato purée
1.4 litres (2½ pints) vegetable stock (page 12)
175 g (6 oz) dried red kidney beans, soaked overnight and drained
2 bay leaves
salt

For garnish
30 ml (2 tablespoons) chopped fresh chives

Melt the margarine in a pan and fry the onions, garlic and celery over moderate heat for 5 minutes, stirring frequently. Stir in the chilli powder – a little at a time if you are not sure how strong your palate is! Let it mellow for 2 minutes, then stir in the tomato purée and gradually pour on the stock. Add the kidney beans and the bay leaves, cover and bring to the boil. Boil rapidly for 15 minutes. Lower the heat and simmer for 2 hours. Before serving, discard the bay leaves and season with salt. Garnish with the chives.
Serves 6

PEA GREEN BOAT

25 g (1 oz) margarine
1 large onion, peeled and sliced

1 clove garlic, peeled and crushed
225 g (8 oz) dried green peas, soaked overnight and
    drained
1.4 litres (2½ pints) vegetable stock (page 12)
2 bay leaves
2 medium potatoes, peeled and diced
2 stalks celery, thinly sliced
2 small leeks, thinly sliced
2 medium carrots, thinly sliced
salt and pepper
50 g (2 oz) Edam cheese, diced

For garnish
garlic croûtons (page 30)

Melt the margarine in a pan and fry the onion and garlic
over moderate heat for 3–4 minutes, stirring once or twice.
Add the green peas, stock and bay leaves and stir well.
Cover, bring to the boil and simmer for 30 minutes. Add the
potatoes and cook for a further 30 minutes. Stir well to break
up the potatoes.

Now add the celery, leeks and carrots, season with salt and
pepper and simmer for a further 15 minutes. Discard the bay
leaves, taste the soup and add more seasoning if needed – it
shouldn't be too bland. Stir in the cheese cubes and scatter
the croûtons on top just as you serve.
Serves 6

BROWN RICE AND LEMON SOUP

It is especially important to use stock with a really strong
flavour, as there are few other distractions in this recipe. If
necessary, boil down the stock to concentrate the flavour.

2.3 litres (4 pints) well-flavoured vegetable stock (page 12)
100 g (4 oz) brown rice
salt

1 handful mixed fresh herbs
grated rind and juice of 2 lemons
3 eggs
15 ml (1 tablespoon) water
pepper

For garnish
60 ml (4 tablespoons) blanched split almonds

Bring the stock to the boil, add the rice, salt, herbs and
grated lemon rind and stir well. Bring to the boil again,
cover and simmer for 40 minutes.

Meanwhile, in a basin beat the eggs until they are frothy
and then stir in the lemon juice and water. Add about 60 ml
(4 tablespoons) of the stock and mix well. Remove the pan of
boiling stock from the heat. Set aside for a minute or so – the
soup mustn't be boiling at this point – then stir in the lemon
mixture; season with more salt if needed and with pepper.
Scatter on the almonds just before serving.
Serves 8

LEEK AND MUSHROOM SOUP

1.4 litres (2½ pints) vegetable stock (page 12)
1 large onion, peeled and thinly sliced
2 large carrots, sliced
4 stalks celery, sliced
1 bouquet garni
15 ml (1 tablespoon) chopped fresh thyme, or parsley
salt
100 g (4 oz) button mushrooms, thinly sliced
4 spring onions, peeled and thinly sliced
2 small leeks, well washed and thinly sliced
30 ml (2 tablespoons) soy sauce
pepper

For garnish
carrot 'flowers' (pages 52-3)

Increase the flavour of the stock by simmering it in a covered pan with the onion, carrot, celery and bouquet garni for 1 hour. Strain and discard the vegetables and herbs.

Return the stock to the pan. Add the fresh herb, salt, mushrooms, spring onions and leeks, bring to the boil and simmer for 5 minutes. Stir in the soy sauce, season with salt and pepper and simmer for a further 5 minutes. Garnish with the carrot 'flowers'.

Serves 4-6

GAZPACHO

Serve this chilled and poured over tinkling ice cubes – it's as refreshing as a salad.

    4 hard-boiled eggs
    4 cloves garlic, crushed
    10 ml (2 teaspoons) mustard powder
    a large pinch of cayenne pepper
    5 ml (1 teaspoon) rock salt
    90 ml (6 tablespoons) olive oil
    100 g (4 oz) button mushrooms, thinly sliced
    1 large cucumber, peeled, seeded and diced
    2 red peppers, seeded and thinly sliced
    8 spring onions, peeled and thinly sliced
    30 ml (2 tablespoons) lemon juice
    30 ml (2 tablespoons) tomato purée
    1.4 litres (2½ pints) tomato juice, chilled
    60 ml (4 tablespoons) wholewheat breadcrumbs
    30 ml (2 tablespoons) chopped fresh parsley
    30 ml (2 tablespoons) chopped fresh chives

For garnish
45 ml (3 tablespoons) soured cream
a pinch of cayenne pepper

For serving
garlic croûtons (page 30)

Scoop the yolks from the eggs. Thinly slice the whites and set aside to use for garnish. Mash the yolks in a large bowl and stir in the garlic, mustard, cayenne and salt. Mix to a paste and gradually stir in the oil.

Stir the mushrooms into this dressing until they are thoroughly coated with oil. Stir in the cucumber, peppers and onions and mix well.

Mix together in a bowl the lemon juice, tomato purée and tomato juice and pour the mixture over the vegetables. Stir well, cover and chill for at least 1 hour. Stir in the breadcrumbs and herbs; taste and add more seasoning if needed.

Pour the soup over the ice in the bowls, garnish with the soured cream and egg whites and sprinkle with a little cayenne pepper for colour. Hand the croûtons separately.
Serves 6

SPICED BANANA SOUP

350 g (12 oz) ripe bananas
30 ml (2 tablespoons) lemon juice
25 g (1 oz) margarine
2 medium onions, peeled and finely chopped
10 ml (2 teaspoons) mild curry powder
2.5 ml (½ teaspoon) ground fennel seeds
10 ml (2 teaspoons) wholewheat semolina
850 ml (1½ pints) vegetable stock (page 12)
salt and pepper
60 ml (4 tablespoons) plain yoghurt

For the topping
4 bran crispbreads, crushed
60 ml (4 tablespoons) chopped walnuts
25 g (1 oz) margarine

Liquidize the bananas with the lemon juice. Melt the margarine in the pan, fry the onions over moderate heat for 2–3 minutes, then stir in the curry powder and fennel. Cook for 1 minute, then stir in the semolina. Add the banana pulp, stirring all the time, then gradually pour on the stock. Season with salt and pepper, cover the pan and bring to the boil. Simmer for 10–15 minutes. Taste and adjust the seasoning if needed. Stir in the yoghurt just before serving.

To make the topping, fry the crispbread crumbs and walnuts in the margarine over moderate heat for 4–5 minutes, stirring frequently, until the crumbs are dry. Scatter over the soup just before serving.

Serves 4

* Make the crumb topping in larger quantities to store. Cool and place in an airtight container. For a variation, use other nuts – cashews, hazelnuts and almonds are all good.

ICED RASPBERRY SOUP

    50 g (2 oz) light Muscovado sugar
    300 ml ($\frac{1}{2}$ pint) water
    1 stick cinnamon
    750 g ($1\frac{1}{2}$ lb) raspberries, hulled
    150 ml ($\frac{1}{4}$ pint) red wine
    150 ml ($\frac{1}{4}$ pint) soured cream

For garnish
30 ml (2 tablespoons) blanched almonds, split and toasted

Place the sugar, water and cinnamon in a pan and stir over low heat to dissolve the sugar, then bring to the boil. Set aside to cool, then remove the cinnamon stick.

Liquidize the syrup, raspberries and wine in a blender. Chill in a covered container in the refrigerator. Stir in half the soured cream. Swirl the remaining cream on top and, just before serving, scatter on the almonds.

Crunchy muesli or honey biscuits are a lovely accompaniment.

Serves 4

* Other berry fruits such as gooseberries or blackberries make good soups too. They're all up-beat, interesting and fibre-full first courses.

APRICOT AND BUTTERMILK SOUP

One of those adaptable recipes – you can serve it before or after the main course. It's slightly sweet, slightly sour and very refreshing.

350 g (12 oz) dried apricots
1.7 litres (3 pints) water
1 stick cinnamon
2 lemons
30 ml (2 tablespoons) thick honey
25 g (1 oz) wholewheat flour
300 ml (½ pint) buttermilk, chilled

For serving
45–60 ml (3–4 tablespoons) melon seeds
60 ml (4 tablespoons) sultanas

Soak the apricots overnight in the water, then add the cinnamon, strips of lemon peel, lemon juice and honey. Place in a saucepan, cover, bring to the boil and simmer for 1 hour. Remove the cinnamon and lemon peel and liquidize the soup in a blender.

Stir a little of the resulting apricot purée into the flour to make a smooth paste, then gradually mix in the remainder. Place in the clean saucepan, stir over low heat for 5 minutes, then cool and chill.

When the soup is cold, beat in the buttermilk until it is well blended. Serve chilled, scattered with the melon seeds and sultanas.
Serves 6–8

* You can use other dried orchard fruits in the same way – try apple rings mixed with peaches, pears or prunes.

CROÛTONS

Add texture and fibre to your soups with a whole repertoire of flavoured croûtons. These can be stored perfectly in a lidded jar or in the freezer, ready to serve with soups or to be scattered on salads, vegetables or baked dishes. You'll wonder how you ever managed without them!

Basic croûtons
      50 g (2 oz) margarine
      8 × 12-mm (½-in) thick slices from large wholewheat loaf
      salt and pepper

Cut the bread into cubes. Melt the margarine in a frying-pan. Add the bread cubes and stir rapidly so that they brown evenly. When they are dry and golden brown in colour, turn them on to kitchen paper to remove excess fat and season at once with salt and pepper. Serve hot or cold, but allow them to cool completely before storing.

Garlic croûtons
Add 2–3 crushed cloves of garlic to the bread when frying and toss in garlic salt and pepper.

Herb croûtons
Toss the croûtons straight from the kitchen paper into 30 ml (2 tablespoons) chopped fresh herbs (such as parsley, thyme or mint, or a mixture) and toss well to coat them thoroughly.

Seed croûtons
Toss the fried cubes in 30 ml (2 tablespoons) celery or sesame seeds or lightly crushed fennel or sunflower seeds.

Spiced croûtons
Toss the cubes after frying in 10–15 ml (2–3 teaspoons) curry powder or ground coriander.

Orange or lemon croûtons
Toss the cubes in 15–30 ml (1–2 tablespoons) grated orange or lemon rind. Orange-flavoured croûtons are specially good with carrot or potato soup; lemon ones give an interesting lift to creamed artichoke or celeriac.

Nut croûtons
Yet another way to add fibre. Toss the croûtons in 45–60 ml (3–4 tablespoons) ground walnuts, almonds, cashews or whatever nuts of your choice.

Cheese croûtons
Sorry, no more fibre but lots of added flavour. Toss the croûtons in 45–60 ml (3–4 tablespoons) very finely grated cheese – Parmesan is ideal.

2   Salads

Salads are the forte of vegetarian eating – and of high-fibre eating, too. Crisp raw vegetables prepared at the last minute – not left to stand about for hours, losing nutrients the while – can make the most attractive and appetizing of mixed dishes, and form a vital part of a healthy diet.

Their appeal is first and foremost visual, so careful preparation is important. Choose only the best and freshest of foods for your salads – slightly older cousins can be consigned to the soup- or stock-pot – and be prepared constantly to improvise with seasonal produce. Variety is the very spice of salads.

A glance at the fibre table (beginning on page 266) will remind you which salad ingredients are highest in fibre. High-fibre salads don't mean a plateful of lettuce leaves and a spoonful of bran, but rather a plate lined with salad greens and piled high with munchy, crunchy sticks and slices of colourful fruit and vegetables.

Add dried fruits, seeds and nuts to your salads and dressings and you increase enormously the fibre content: dates with cabbage and apple; sultanas with fennel and orange; spinach with sesame seeds; beetroot and red cabbage with brazil nuts – the combinations are so delicious and they're good for you. Also, when you have a couple of spoonfuls of dried pulses left over – lentils, chick peas, kidney beans – toss those with fresh salad vegetables and up goes the fibre count again.

Some people hold that any salad is only as good as its dressing, and a few others say that a good salad needs no such adornment. My own feeling is that a light dressing with a good, subtle flavour draws the ingredients of a mixed salad together. If you agree, make a basic vinaigrette dressing (page 54) and store at room temperature (not refrigerated) in a lidded container. Measure out as much as you need for each salad and occasionally whisk in extra flavouring in the form of powdered spices – curry, paprika, cayenne; chopped fresh herbs; orange or lemon juice, grated fruit rind; crushed garlic and finely chopped onions or shallots. For a change, and for a smooth cream-and-green consistency, liquidize vinaigrette dressing and herbs in a blender.

If you are serving a salad that is not specially high in fibre, compensate by whisking some bran into the dressing – it's amazing what you can get away with! – or stir in a high-fibre ingredient such as grated horseradish. Try diluting a dried pulse dip by whisking in vegetable oil until you have a smooth, creamy liquid. Season the dressing well with salt and pepper and stir in chopped fresh herbs.

To increase the protein content, crumble cheese like Greek feta, Wensleydale, Stilton or Danish blue into vinaigrette dressing, or scatter cubes of cheese over the salad and garnish it with a few drops of oil.

Garnishes can add enormously to salad eye-appeal. Choose from sprigs of watercress or herbs; black or green olives; tomatoes, oranges, lemons and hard-boiled eggs in wedges or slices; fresh vegetable crudités (page 52); or even flowers – nasturtiums, wild flowers of all kinds, single white chrysanthemums, tiny sprays of flowering herbs all add a touch of the exotic. And why not!

COTTAGE GARDEN SALAD

With eggs, vegetables, salad greens, herbs and olives, it's a sparkling meal in itself.

225 g (8 oz) new potatoes
225 g (8 oz) French beans, topped and tailed
450 g (1 lb) broad beans, shelled
salt
1 small endive, washed and dried
225-g (8-oz) can artichoke hearts, drained
45 ml (3 tablespoons) chopped fresh herbs, e.g. parsley,
  marjoram, thyme
4 hard-boiled eggs, quartered
4 medium tomatoes, quartered
2 canned pimentos, drained and thinly sliced
75 g (3 oz) black olives
25 g (1 oz) stuffed green olives

For the dressing
120 ml (8 tablespoons) vinaigrette dressing (page 54)
15 ml (1 tablespoon) bran
1 clove garlic, peeled and halved

First prepare the dressing. Shake or mix the ingredients vigorously, and season to taste.

Cook the potatoes, French beans and broad beans separately in boiling, salted water – or steam them – until they are just tender. Drain, dunk them in cold water to prevent over-cooking, then drain again. Slice the French beans if they are large.

Carefully stir the cooked vegetables together. Remove the garlic from the dressing and discard. Pour one-third of the dressing over the vegetables, stir to coat them well and leave to cool.

Place the endive leaves in a large shallow dish and, just before serving, pour on half the remaining dressing and toss

to coat the leaves thoroughly. Stir the artichoke hearts and herbs into the cooled vegetables and pile them on to the endive. Arrange a ring of alternate egg and tomato wedges around the outside. Criss-cross strips of pimento over the vegetables and scatter on the olives. Pour the remaining dressing over the salad to make it glisten.
Serves 4

NUTTY SLAW

A salad that hits the jackpot for fibre – and for texture, colour and flavour too.

  1 small white cabbage, shredded
  2 large carrots, grated
  4 stalks celery, thinly sliced
  1 small onion, peeled and finely chopped
  2 dessert apples, cored and chopped
  15 ml (1 tablespoon) lemon juice
  100 g (4 oz) walnut halves
  100 g (4 oz) cashew nuts
  50 g (2 oz) stoned dried dates, chopped

  For the dressing
  75 ml (5 tablespoons) oil
  15 ml (1 tablespoon) bran
  grated rind and juice of 1 orange
  salt and pepper

  For garnish
  1 bunch watercress sprigs

Toss together the cabbage, carrots, celery and onion. Toss the apples in the lemon juice and stir them with the nuts and dates into the vegetables.

Mix the dressing ingredients together, taste and add more seasoning if needed. About 1 hour before serving, pour the

dressing over the salad and stir to coat it thoroughly.
Garnish with the watercress.
Serves 4–6

SPROUTING BEAN GLORY

Whether you grow your own or buy them, crunchy fresh
beansprouts make an exciting salad.

8 radishes, thinly sliced
100 g (4 oz) button mushrooms, thinly sliced
4 stalks celery, thinly sliced
4 spring onions, peeled and thinly sliced
225 g (8 oz) beansprouts, washed and drained
2 large carrots, grated
1 green pepper, seeded and thinly sliced
75 ml (5 tablespoons) vinaigrette dressing (page 54)

For serving
spinach or lettuce leaves

Toss together all the vegetable ingredients. Pour the dressing
over the salad and toss to coat it thoroughly. Cover and set
aside at room temperature for about 30 minutes. To serve,
pile the salad on to a bed of spinach or lettuce leaves.
Serves 4

SPINACH AND BEANSPROUT TOSS-UP

Very good with egg dishes such as omelettes or soufflés.

1 small cucumber, cut into matchstick strips
225 g (8 oz) beansprouts, washed and drained
8–12 young spinach leaves, washed and torn into pieces
50 g (2 oz) cashew nuts
50 g (2 oz) seedless raisins

For the dressing
90 ml (6 tablespoons) vinaigrette dressing (page 54)
a few drops of soy sauce

Toss the salad ingredients together. Mix the dressing with
the soy sauce and be sure it's seasoned to your liking. Just
before serving, toss the salad in the dressing.
Serves 4

SPICY LEEK AND BEAN SALAD

175 g (6 oz) cooked dried beans (e.g. flageolets, haricot,
    kidney)
4 medium leeks, well washed and thinly sliced
1 medium onion, peeled and finely chopped
1 large carrot, thinly sliced

For the dressing
105 ml (7 tablespoons) vinaigrette dressing (page 54)
15 ml (1 tablespoon) bran
1 canned pimento, drained and chopped
salt
1 clove garlic, peeled and crushed

For serving
lettuce leaves

For garnish
2 hard-boiled eggs, sliced

Mix all the dressing ingredients together by stirring or
shaking vigorously in a suitable container, or by liquidizing
in a blender. Mix together the beans, leeks, onion and
carrot, pour on the dressing, cover and leave at room
temperature for at least 1 hour.

Just before serving, line a dish with the lettuce leaves, pile
on the salad and garnish with the egg slices.
Serves 4

SWEET SPINACH

The dried fruits waft away any hint of bitterness in the spinach.

> 450 g (1 lb) young spinach leaves
> 2 bunches watercress sprigs
> ½ small cucumber, cut into matchstick strips
> 100 g (4 oz) dried apricots, quartered
> 175 g (6 oz) stoned dried dates, chopped
>
> *For the dressing*
> 75 ml (5 tablespoons) oil
> 30 ml (2 tablespoons) orange juice
> 15 ml (1 tablespoon) clear honey
> salt and pepper

Thoroughly wash the spinach, discard the stalks and pat the leaves dry (or use a salad spinner). Tear each leaf into 2 or 3 pieces. Toss together the spinach, watercress, cucumber, apricots and dates.

Beat the dressing ingredients together until the honey has dissolved. Just before serving, pour over the salad and toss thoroughly.

Serves 4–6

FENNEL AND ORANGE SIDER

A crisp, refreshing 'side salad' to serve with egg and cheese dishes. It makes a sparky first course, too.

> 2 medium heads fennel, very thinly sliced
> 3 oranges, peeled and segmented
> 4 spring onions, peeled and sliced
> 30 ml (2 tablespoons) sultanas
> 30 ml (2 tablespoons) walnut halves
> 2 bunches watercress sprigs

For the dressing
75 ml (5 tablespoons) vinaigrette dressing (page 54)
15 ml (1 tablespoon) bran
15 ml (1 tablespoon) fennel seeds
5 ml (1 teaspoon) orange juice
5 ml (1 teaspoon) grated orange rind

For serving
1 firm lettuce, cut into 8 wedges

Toss the dressing ingredients together. Mix together the salad ingredients, add the dressing and toss well. Just before serving, spoon the salad over the lettuce wedges.
Serves 4

MANGE-TOUT MIMOSA

A luxury summer vegetable, served cold as part of an hors d'oeuvre, or as a main-dish accompaniment.

450 g (1 lb) mange-tout peas, topped and tailed
salt
15 ml (1 tablespoon) lemon juice
5 ml (1 teaspoon) light Muscovado sugar

For the dressing
90 ml (6 tablespoons) vinaigrette dressing (page 54)
30 ml (2 tablespoons) chopped fresh parsley
2 small gherkins, finely chopped
1 small onion, peeled and finely chopped

For garnish
4 hard-boiled eggs

Put the peas in just enough boiling water to cover them. Add the salt, lemon juice and sugar and cook for 10–12 minutes, until they are just tender. Drain the peas and set them aside to cool.

Mix the dressing, pour it over the peas, toss to coat them well and set aside for about 30 minutes.

Chop the egg whites and yolks separately and very finely and, just before serving, arrange them in yellow and white lines across the salad.

Serves 4

---

* The same treatment flatters very young French beans, too.

SALAD CARLOS

2 large, ripe avocados
spinach leaves
1 grapefruit, peeled and segmented
8 stalks celery, thinly sliced
100 g (4 oz) button mushrooms, thinly sliced
50 g (2 oz) stuffed green olives, sliced

For the dressing
75 ml (5 tablespoons) vinaigrette dressing (page 54)
5 ml (1 teaspoon) grated grapefruit rind
30 ml (2 tablespoons) pumpkin seeds

Mix the dressing in a bowl. Peel, halve and slice the avocados straight into it so that they don't discolour. Line a dish with the spinach leaves and arrange on them a ring of alternating avocado and grapefruit segments. Toss the celery, mushrooms and olives in the remaining dressing and pile them in the centre.

Serves 4

BREATHTAKING SALAD

It's a slaw with a difference – the horseradish dressing.

225 g (8 oz) firm white cabbage, shredded
2 large carrots, thinly sliced
3 dessert apples, cored and thinly sliced

For the dressing
150 ml (¼ pint) plain yoghurt, chilled
15–30 ml (1–2 tablespoons) grated horseradish (amount depends on pungency)
30 ml (2 tablespoons) oil
salt

For serving
lettuce leaves

For garnish
8 large radishes, cut into 'roses' (page 54)

First prepare the dressing. Beat the yoghurt, horseradish and oil to make a smooth sauce and season with salt. Toss together the cabbage, carrots and apples and stir in the dressing. Pile the salad on to a bed of lettuce leaves and arrange the radishes to garnish.
Serves 4

VALENTINE SALAD

A very substantial salad to serve with a light main dish.

225 g (8 oz) cooked beetroot, skinned and cut into matchstick strips
225 g (8 oz) red cabbage, shredded
2 dessert apples, cored and thinly sliced
50 g (2 oz) dried figs, thinly sliced
25 g (1 oz) brazil nuts, sliced

For the dressing
75 ml (5 tablespoons) vinaigrette dressing (page 54)
15 ml (1 tablespoon) buttermilk or plain yoghurt

The method is simple. Toss the saladings together. Mix the dressing ingredients. Then toss the two together.
Serves 6

NEW-WAY POTATOES

1 kg (2¼ lb) new potatoes
salt
60 ml (4 tablespoons) seedless raisins

For the dressing
75 ml (5 tablespoons) vinaigrette dressing (page 54)
5 ml (1 teaspoon) mild curry powder
15 ml (1 tablespoon) bran
30 ml (2 tablespoons) chopped fresh parsley
30 ml (2 tablespoons) fenugreek seeds

Cook the potatoes in their skins in boiling, salted water for 12–15 minutes, until they are just tender. Drain them.

Have the dressing ready mixed – all the ingredients just tossed together – so that you can pour it over the hot potatoes. Leave them to cool, turning them in the dressing occasionally, then stir in the raisins.
Serves 4–6

GREEN CHOICE WITH BANANA DRESSING

When you choose a crisp, cool selection of green saladings, hide the fibre in a memorable dressing. It's good, too, with all cabbage-based salads.

1 'salad bowl' lettuce
2 heads chicory

a few young spinach leaves
a few young nasturtium leaves (optional)
175 g (6 oz) firm white cabbage, shredded

For the dressing
2 bananas
30 ml (2 tablespoons) bran
150 ml (¼ pint) apple juice
5 ml (1 teaspoon) oil
salt and pepper

For garnish
100 g (4 oz) unsalted peanuts

Wash and dry the salad leaves and tear them into small pieces. Toss them in a bowl with the cabbage. Liquidize the dressing ingredients in a blender and, just before serving, pour over the salad and toss well. Scatter with the peanuts.
Serves 4

CABBAGE AND DATE BOWL

175 g (6 oz) firm white cabbage, shredded
175 g (6 oz) red cabbage, shredded
4 stalks celery, thinly sliced
225 g (8 oz) stoned dried dates, chopped

For the dressing
30 ml (2 tablespoons) concentrated orange juice
150 ml (¼ pint) plain yoghurt
45 ml (3 tablespoons) chopped fresh chives

For serving
1 small cucumber, thinly sliced

Another quick one! In a bowl, toss together the cabbage, celery and dates. Mix together the dressing ingredients, pour

over the salad and toss well. Arrange in a dish with an outer
ring of overlapping cucumber slices.
Serves 4

CAULIFLOWER AND SOYA SURPRISE

1 small cauliflower
salt
100 g (4 oz) cooked dried soya beans
4 medium courgettes, thinly sliced

For the dressing
120 ml (8 tablespoons) vinaigrette dressing (page 54)
15 ml (1 tablespoon) orange juice
100 g (4 oz) seedless raisins

Cut the cauliflower into small florets and steam over salted
water for 5 minutes, or until it is barely tender. Plunge it into
cold water to prevent further cooking, then drain thoroughly
and allow to cool. (Waste not! Reserve the cauliflower leaves
and stalks to make a creamy soup – they soon whizz up in a
liquidizer. Or grate them raw for a salad – great with
peanuts.)

Toss together the cauliflower, beans and courgettes. Mix
the dressing with the orange juice and stir in the raisins.
Pour over the vegetables and toss gently until well blended.
Serves 4

* Stacks of fibre in this dressing – try it with all kinds of
other salads. It's especially good with cabbage-based varieties.

ITALIAN BREAD SALAD

Here's a way to use up several-days-old bread – unusually.

175 g (6 oz) wholewheat bread
60 ml (4 tablespoons) olive oil

15 ml (1 tablespoon) lemon juice
1 small onion, peeled and finely chopped
2 cloves garlic, peeled and finely chopped
75 ml (5 tablespoons) chopped fresh basil
salt and pepper
50 g (2 oz) black olives

For serving
lettuce leaves
8 tomatoes, quartered

Cut the crusts from the bread. Crumble the bread and soak it in water for 20 minutes. Drain in a colander, then tip into a clean tea towel. Roll up the towel and twist the ends in opposite directions to force all the water from the bread.

Mix the now-dry bread with the oil, lemon juice, onion, garlic and basil, season well with salt and pepper and stir in the olives. Pile the salad on to a dish lined with lettuce leaves and arrange the tomatoes in a pattern around the edge.
Serves 4

SPINACH SALAD

For me, this salad is pure vicarious living: it reminds me of long and lazy holidays in Greece.

900 g (2 lb) spinach leaves
salt

For the dressing
75 ml (5 tablespoons) vinaigrette dressing (page 54)
45 ml (3 tablespoons) sesame seeds

Wash the spinach and tear off the stalks and discard. Put the leaves into a pan of salted water, bring to the boil and cook for 5 minutes. Drain very thoroughly – even to the extent of pressing the spinach against the sides of the colander if necessary. You must get it really dry. Leave to cool.

Toss together the dressing and sesame seeds. Pour the dressing over the spinach turning it over and over to coat all the leaves. It's a good accompaniment to eggy dishes.
Serves 4

MUSHROOMS IN RED WINE

Rich, black and delicious, this dish makes a meal alongside a green salad and tomatoes.

45 ml (3 tablespoons) oil
2 large onions, peeled and chopped
2 cloves garlic, peeled and crushed
10 ml (2 teaspoons) cumin seeds
250 ml (9 fl oz) red wine
450 g (1 lb) medium mushrooms, trimmed
15 ml (1 tablespoon) red wine vinegar
30 ml (2 tablespoons) chopped fresh chervil, or parsley
salt and pepper

For garnish
45 ml (3 tablespoons) pumpkin seeds

Heat the oil in a pan and fry the onions, garlic and cumin seeds over moderate heat, stirring, for 3–4 minutes. Pour in the wine, stir well, bring to the boil and fast-boil for 5 minutes, to concentrate the flavours. Add the mushrooms to the stock and simmer for 2 minutes. Stir in the vinegar, bring just to the boil then remove from the heat. Mix in the herb, season with salt and pepper and allow to cool. Scatter with the pumpkin seeds. Serve well chilled, with plenty of bread to soak up the sauce.
Serves 4

* As an alternative, serve the mushrooms hot, poured over rice or pasta, and with a cool green salad to contrast.

BROAD BEAN 'SPOTTED DICK'

  1 kg (2¼ lb) broad beans, shelled
  salt
  75 ml (5 tablespoons) vinaigrette dressing (page 54)
  ½ small cucumber, cut into matchstick strips
  100 g (4 oz) blanched almonds, split and toasted
  30 ml (2 tablespoons) fresh chopped summer savory, or
      parsley

Cook the beans in boiling, salted water for 10-12 minutes,
until they are only just tender. Drain the beans, toss them in
the dressing and set aside to cool. Stir in the cucumber,
almonds and herbs and serve at once – nuts quickly soften.
Serves 4-6

MEXICAN RELISH

This salad goes especially well with Green Choice and
Banana Dressing (page 42)

  4 large heads sweetcorn
  salt
  2 red peppers, seeded and thinly sliced
  30 ml (2 tablespoons) chopped fresh chives
  100 g (4 oz) button mushrooms, thinly sliced
  2 heads chicory
  2 boxes cress

  For serving
  75 ml (5 tablespoons) vinaigrette dressing (page 54)

Cook the sweetcorn in boiling, salted water for 15-20
minutes, until they are tender (older heads will take a little
longer). Drain and cool them, then run a sharp knife
between core and kernels to strip off the seeds. Toss them in
a bowl with the peppers, chives and mushrooms and

then pile the salad on to a bed of chicory leaves. Ring round with the cress.

Pour the dressing over the salad just before serving.
Serves 4

THREE-BEAN SALAD

Salads don't come any higher in fibre than this one. Served with eggs and a green salad it's a substantial meal.

75 g (3 oz) dried chick-peas, soaked overnight and drained
75 g (3 oz) dried red kidney beans, soaked overnight and drained
75 g (3 oz) dried flageolets or white haricot beans, soaked overnight and drained
lettuce leaves, to serve
4 large tomatoes, quartered
about 60 ml (4 tablespoons) black olives
1 bunch watercress sprigs

For the dressing
120 ml (8 tablespoons) vinaigrette dressing (page 54)
2 cloves garlic, peeled and crushed
1 medium onion, peeled and finely chopped

For serving
150 ml (¼ pint) plain yoghurt, chilled
45 ml (3 tablespoons) chopped fresh mint
salt and pepper

Prepare the dressing by tossing together all three ingredients.

Cook the three pulses in separate pans of boiling, unsalted water for 1¼-1½ hours, or until they are just tender. Drain them and while they are still hot, mix each batch separately in the onion and garlic dressing.

Set out the lettuce leaves on a dish and arrange on this bed in separate portions the three pulses. Between each portion place tomato wedges and olives and arrange the watercress sprigs around the edge.

Mix together the yoghurt and mint, season with salt and pepper and serve this dressing separately.
Serves 4-6

LENTIL SALAD

As a first course or part of a cold meal, lentil salad is filling and tasty. Help its eye-appeal by serving it in fruit shells.

350 g (12 oz) green lentils, washed
850 ml (1½ pints) water
a handful of parsley stalks
30 ml (2 tablespoons) oil
1 medium onion, peeled and finely chopped
1 clove garlic, peeled and crushed
30 ml (2 tablespoons) sweet sherry
salt and pepper
15 ml (1 tablespoon) lemon juice
4 spring onions, peeled and thinly sliced
45 ml (3 tablespoons) chopped fresh parsley

For serving
4 half-grapefruit or large half-orange shells

For garnish
watercress sprigs

Put the lentils, water and parsley into a pan, bring to the boil, cover and simmer for 50 minutes to 1 hour, or until the lentils are soft. Discard the parsley.

Heat the oil in a small pan and fry the onion and garlic over moderate heat, stirring occasionally, for 4 minutes. Stir this mixture, the lemon juice and sherry into the lentils and beat well, still over the heat, until it is smooth. Set aside to cool completely.

Season the salad with salt and pepper and stir in the spring onion and chopped parsley. Spoon the salad into the 'fruit bowls' and garnish with the watercress sprigs. This dish is eaten with a teaspoon.

Serves 4

CHICK-PEA PASTE

Here is one of those wonderful Greek-style dips to serve with hot pitta bread or fingers of toast. And to enjoy with relish!

175 g (6 oz) dried chick-peas, soaked overnight and drained
45 ml (3 tablespoons) tahini paste
30 ml (2 tablespoons) olive oil
30 ml (2 tablespoons) lemon juice
2 cloves garlic, peeled and crushed
125 ml (4 fl oz) water
60 ml (4 tablespoons) parsley, flat-leafed if available
salt and pepper

Cook the chick-peas in plenty of boiling, unsalted water for 2½ hours, or until they are tender. Drain, and set aside 30 ml (2 tablespoons) of the chick-peas.

Put the tahini paste, oil, lemon juice, garlic and water into a blender, add the chick-peas and blend to make a smooth paste, adding a little more water if necessary. Stir in half the parsley and season well – be generous as you need to offset the blandness of the pulses. Stir in the reserved chick-peas and pile the salad into a dish. Dribble on a little extra olive oil to make the dish glisten and sprinkle with the remaining parsley.

Serve the salad with hot wholewheat pitta bread or fingers of wholewheat toast.

Serves 4

BUTTER BEAN DIP

With a colourful selection of crudités, those fresh-vegetable dipsticks, this is as attractive a first course as you could muster.

175 g (6 oz) butter beans, soaked overnight and drained
105 ml (7 tablespoons) olive oil
25 ml (1½ tablespoons) red wine vinegar
2 cloves garlic, peeled and crushed
75 ml (5 tablespoons) water
salt and pepper

For serving
a pinch of cayenne pepper
a selection of crudités (page 52). Choose from red and green peppers, carrot, cauliflower, spring onion, parsnip, radish

Cook the beans in plenty of boiling, unsalted water for about 1¼ hours, or until they are tender. Drain them.

Put the oil, vinegar, garlic and water into a blender, add the beans and blend to a smooth purée, adding a little more water if needed. Season the purée well with salt and pepper and pile it into a bowl. Sprinkle with a little cayenne, for colour and pungency. Surround the salad with an arrangement of suitably prepared crisp, fresh vegetables to use as dipsticks.
Serves 4

AUBERGINE AND YOGHURT DIP

With pitta bread or crudités, this is a first course with all the flavour of the Middle East. With lots more bread and a green salad it's a simple meal.

2 large aubergines, about 225 g (8 oz) each
60 ml (4 tablespoons) olive oil
2 cloves garlic, peeled and crushed
45 ml (3 tablespoons) bran
30 ml (2 tablespoons) lemon juice
about 225 ml (8 fl oz) plain yoghurt
30 ml (2 tablespoons) chopped fresh chervil, or parsley
salt and pepper

Grill the aubergines under a medium-hot grill for about 25 minutes, turning them often. They will be ready when the skin turns black and blisters and the flesh softens. As soon as they are cool enough to handle, peel off the skins.

Mash the aubergine flesh in a bowl with the oil, garlic, bran and lemon juice – or whizz them together in a blender. Beat in just enough of the yoghurt to make a soft paste, stir in the herb and add lots of salt and pepper.
Serves 6

CRUDITÉS

Crudités are raw (or sometimes very slightly cooked) vegetables cut into convenient bite-sized pieces or decorative shapes. These dipsticks are the healthiest possible accompaniment to soft, creamy pâtés and cheese and vegetable dips; the fancy shapes, whether they are celery or spring onion 'frills' or carrot 'flowers', can be used to garnish soups, salads, dips or main dishes.

Choose fresh, tender young vegetables and be really selective. (Those not suitable can form part of the soup or pâté.) Wash, dry and if necessary scrub root vegetables but don't peel them.

Carrots For dipsticks, cut the carrots into quarters or eighths lengthways, then into about 6.5-cm (2½-in) lengths. To make 'flower' shapes or clubs, diamonds, hearts or spades, for that matter – cut into very thin slices then punch out the shape, using aspic cutters. It's easier if you partly cook the carrots first. They're super for garnishing soups, the tops of pâtés – using parsley stalks and herb leaves to make a 'bouquet' – or to decorate individual salad plates.

Cauliflower Cut into small or medium florets and use these as dipsticks. The tiny florets can also be used to garnish cold dishes, such as vegetable pâtés.

Celery Cut thin dipsticks. Or, from the larger stalks, cut 4–5-cm (1½–2-in) lengths and fill the hollows with cream cheese or, say, aubergine pâté. To make decorative 'frills', cut young, thin stalks in half lengthways, then into 7.5-cm (3-in) lengths. Make slits from one end reaching half way down, then soak in ice-cold water. The thin strips will open up and curl round to give a frilled umbrella effect.

Cucumber Make dipsticks, as for carrots. To make cones, cut the cucumber into thin slices; cut each slice from the outside to the centre and overlap the two cut edges to form a cone. Or make cucumber boats – cut the cucumber in half lengthways and scoop out the seeds. Fill the hollow with a dip or pâté and cut the whole into bite-sized lengths.

Cucumber is very low in fibre so compensate with a beany dip such as Butter bean dip (page 51) or Chick-pea paste (page 50).

Mushrooms Trim the stalk end then cut through cap and stalk in thick slices. An overlapping line of these characteristic shapes makes an attractive garnish to vegetable loaves or pastry dishes.

Parsnips Make dipsticks as for carrots. Toss in lemon juice to preserve the colour.

Peppers Cut away the stalk, pith and seeds. Cut into dipsticks, or cut through the peppers to make rings – effective arranged on top of salads. Or stamp out flower and other shapes, as for carrots.

Radishes To make a radish 'rose', cut a series of criss-cross slits in the top and soak in ice-cold water for 2 hours. Or, more immediate (no soaking), cut long radishes in half; make slits through from the outside almost to the centre, each one at right-angles to the last. Pull apart and *voilà* – a 'water-lily'! For 'fans', slice nearly through all along the length and soak similarly. Or just slice. Red on the outside and white inside, they add crisp, clear colour.

Spring onions Trim off root and outer layers. Cut into lengths and proceed as for celery 'frills'.

VINAIGRETTE DRESSING

This is a basic French dressing, which can be varied in all manner of ways. Use cider, white or red wine or tarragon vinegar; olive, sunflower, soya, walnut or other vegetable oils – each has its own distinctive flavour.

    5 ml (1 teaspoon) mustard powder
    5 ml (1 teaspoon) light Muscovado sugar
    300 ml (½ pint) oil
    90–120 ml (6–8 tablespoons) cider vinegar or other vinegar
    salt and pepper

Stir together the mustard and sugar and gradually beat in the oil, then the vinegar. Season with salt and pepper and shake or beat thoroughly. Store in a lidded container at room temperature. Shake or whisk vigorously before using.

* For a lemony dressing, replace part of the vinegar with lemon juice.

MAYONNAISE

2 egg yolks, at room temperature
300 ml (½ pint) olive oil
15 ml (1 tablespoon) lemon juice
salt and pepper

Beat the egg yolks until they are creamy. Add the oil drop by drop, beating all the time, then gradually pour it in a steady stream, still beating. Beat in the lemon juice and season with salt and pepper.

Alternatively, put the egg yolks into a blender, switch on and slowly pour in the oil; when it has all been absorbed add the lemon juice. Season with salt and pepper. Store in a refrigerator.

3   Rice and Other Grains

Rice and all the other whole grain cereal – barley, corn, millet, oats, rye, wheat – have been the staple diet of non-industrialized and so-called under-developed nations for centuries: countries to which, remember, our modern Western dietary ailments are virtually unknown. At last this fact seems to have been acknowledged, and the great pendulum of progress in the field of food technology has been given a mighty shove backwards. Wholegrain cereals are much more readily available now in ordinary shops and supermarkets, and much more widely used, in relation to their processed equivalents, than was the case ten or even five years ago.

Vegetarians have always recognized the high nutritional value of these foods and eaten them in fair quantity and enormous variety as an important source of protein, fat, vitamins and other nutrients. Now, with the overwhelming medical evidence, we can add dietary fibre to that list of very good reasons for enjoying these wholesome, *natural* foods.

Cooked and served simply, with a nutty texture and modesty of flavour, grains are the perfect accompaniment to highly spiced or well-flavoured foods – curry and rice being the prime example. Add vegetables, herbs, spices, fruit or nuts to the grain, as in a pilaff or risotto, and they become an integral part of the main dish, endlessly variable and infinitely enjoyable. Add the grains to a soup or casserole and they hide their identity, but contribute bulk, satisfaction and 'goodness'. And if an experiment in cooking grains ever goes wrong and you produce an unappetizing mass – it *can* happen, the first time! – all is far from lost. I whizz them up in the blender to thicken and fortify a soup, and a new recipe is born!

Rice

Natural unprocessed rice is available in long-grain and short-grain types. And, unlike processed rice, it is the short, fat grains that are generally considered easier to cook so that they remain separate and 'fluffy'. There are two basic ways to cook rice, and indeed other grains too. One is by boiling in a large quantity of water or stock for 40–45 minutes (rice); drain into a colander, refresh and separate the grains by running hot water through, then drain again. The other is by a method which starts as simmering and, as the liquid is absorbed, ends as steaming; this can be done on top of the stove or in the oven.

For the second method, you need about twice the volume of liquid to rice. The trick is to measure the rice into a millilitre (fluid ounce) measure, read off the scale and then measure out double that amount of liquid. (As a guide, 225 g (8 oz) of rice measures 300 ml ($\frac{1}{2}$ pint) on the scale, so absorbs 600 ml (1 pint) of liquid.) Put the rice into a wide-based pan (on top of the cooker, I always use a lidded frying-pan) add salt and liquid – water, stock, cider, even some wine if you wish – and bring to the boil. Stir the rice, lower to minimum heat, cover the pan and set the timer for 40 minutes (it might take 45). Nervous cooks stir the rice once or twice during cooking, others wouldn't dream of it. By the time the liquid is absorbed the rice should be just tender.

Here's another tip, and it applies to cooking all grains by this method. The less liquid you add, the shorter will be the cooking time (unless you want to burn 'your pan!) and therefore the tougher will be the grains. The more liquid added, the longer it will take to be absorbed and the more time the grains will have to soften – and end up a mass if you're not careful. Adjust the proportion of liquid slightly up or down of the one-to-two ratio to suit your preference. One person's *al dente* is another person's bullets!

For more flavour, toss the rice in melted butter, margarine or a vegetable oil before adding the liquid and setting to cook. Fry flavouring vegetables such as onion, garlic and celery first; stir in ground spices at this stage, then add the rice and the liquid and set to cook. It all adds personality and individuality, and means that any selection of recipes can be just the tip of the iceberg – an ideas springboard.

Cooked rice is *useable* in so many ways, it's a good idea to cook it in large batches on the one-for-now/one-for-later principle. Use left-over rice for a paella (see page 70), again of infinite variety; for rice cakes which can be breadcrumbed and baked or deep- or shallow-fried; or for last-minute soup doctoring. Cooked rice can be stored in a lidded container in the refrigerator for up to 1 week.

There are much tougher grains than rice which can be used in the same ways. Unprocessed barley, dried corn (maize), oats, rye and wheat all benefit from overnight soaking. Drain them and cook in a large pan of unsalted liquid for the time it takes to soften them – this will depend on the variety, age and so on, probably about 2 hours. Then add salt.

Millet, a much smaller seed, is one of the quickies. Simmer it in slightly more than twice its volume of liquid – 225 g (8 oz) of millet takes up about 700 ml (1¼ pints) of liquid in 25 minutes.

Grains are available in treated forms that take considerably less time to cook; some can be added to flour for pastry, made into crumble fillings and toppings, or – especially in the case of wheat – served as a salad.

Barley
Sometimes called pot barley, this has a tough husk and needs long cooking. It is available in toasted (when it can be eaten 'raw', like nuts) and processed forms. Pearl barley is the polished grain, used to thicken soups and for milk puddings. Barley flour makes a flat, low-rise bread while barley flakes can be eaten raw, in muesli especially.

Corn or maize
The early American food staple, this can be bought fresh or frozen or canned as whole kernels off the cob. Dried corn looks like the animal feed it often is, until it has been long-soaked and long-cooked. One variety of corn makes 'popcorn' – it can be home-roasted or fried and will snap, crackle and pop cheerfully! A variety of white maize produces hominy, which is treated with lye to dissolve the skins. Coarsely ground, this cereal is known as hominy grits and makes a type of porridge. Corn meal, golden yellow, is used for flat breads and tortillas; cornflour is ultra-processed, pure white, dust-fine and used for thickening.

Millet
These small seeds are popular for their short cooking time (as mentioned above) and can be eaten raw. They are available as whole grain, flakes and flour.

Oats
These have the highest protein content of all cereals. Whole oats are in the long-soak, long-cook category. They are also available in toasted form. Fine, medium and coarse grades of oatmeal are used for porridge and baked goods; so too are oat flakes and rolled oats, which are available in two sizes – ordinary and 'jumbo' – both good in muesli. Rolled oats have a fibre content of about 7 per cent.

Cereal bran and germ, added to many dishes for extra

fibre, is usually extracted from wheat, but oatbran and oatgerm, which has an 18 per cent fibre content, is now also marketed.

Rye

This is sold as whole grain, flakes and flour, the latter being used for the heavy grey and black Continental breads; it has a characteristic slightly sour flavour.

Wheat

If so much of our wheat hadn't been processed and robbed of the dietary fibre – the bran and the germ – perhaps this book would never have been written! Wholegrain wheat, from which only the (truly!) inedible husks have been removed, can be used in the ways suggested for rice – it just takes longer to cook. The bran is the inner husk, and is now marketed to put back into our diet what we have thoughtlessly allowed to be taken out. However, with a sensible diet of our own choosing, additional bran should not be necessary. The germ is the embryo, which contains the greater part of the proteins, fat and vitamins. This is available in powdered form. You will find more information on flours in Chapter 11.

Cracked wheat, called burghul or bulghar, is made by soaking the grains, then toasting them until they crack. As such, they're ready-cooked and can be eaten, for example, after short soaking and meticulous drying, in Middle-Eastern-type salads.

Wheat flakes, familiar muesli ingredients, can be eaten raw or, as with other flaked grains, used in baking. Semolina is a fine grain milled from durum wheat, a hard variety; be sure to buy wholewheat semolina, which is just what it says. It's excellent for thickening soups and casseroles; can be ultra-thickened to make a pasta-like paste, the Italian gnocchi; and is good for nursery puddings.

Recipes for grain-based puddings can be found in Chapter 10.

MUESLI BASE (1)

Make your own muesli base in quantity and store it in a lidded container. You can of course add seeds, more nuts and dried fruits too, leaving just fresh fruits or vegetables for the last-minute additions.

225 g (8 oz) rolled oats
50 g (2 oz) stabilized wheatgerm
30 ml (2 tablespoons) sunflower seeds
50 g (2 oz) bran
100 g (4 oz) wheat flakes
100 g (4 oz) jumbo oats
225 g (8 oz) mixed nuts

This is a very basic muesli, just a selection of the 'good grains', and nuts, to stir together and store. Be sure the wheatgerm you buy *is* stabilized, otherwise it loses its freshness if not stored in the refrigerator.
Makes 850 g (1¾ lb)

MUESLI BASE (2)

Completely interchangeable with the foregoing basic muesli – just a different blend of grains and textures.

175 g (6 oz) jumbo oats
100 g (4 oz) oat flakes
100 g (4 oz) wheat flakes
100 g (4 oz) oatbran and oatgerm
50 g (2 oz) millet flakes
225 g (8 oz) mixed nuts
45 ml (3 tablespoons) millet seeds

Mix all the grains, seeds and nuts together and store as an 'undressed' muesli, ready for a variety of additions.
Makes 850 g (1¾ lb)

* Alternatively make it even simpler: four parts of jumbo oats or rolled porridge oats and one part bran, with the added interest of nuts and seeds, makes a good high-fibre muesli base.

DRIED FRUIT MUESLI

You can add the dried fruits of your choice to a muesli base and store the mixture for instant use. Here's one successful combination.

1 recipe Muesli base (1) or (2) (page 61)
100 g (4 oz) seedless raisins
100 g (4 oz) stoned dried dates, sliced
100 g (4 oz) chopped mixed candied peel
100 g (4 oz) dried figs, chopped
50 g (2 oz) dried banana slices
50 g (2 oz) pumpkin seeds

Mix all the ingredients together to distribute the fruit evenly. Serve with chilled plain yoghurt, buttermilk, or unsweetened fruit juices. Try a half-and-half mixture of yoghurt and orange juice, or buttermilk and cloudy apple juice – surprisingly good.
Makes about 1.4 kg (3 lb)

FRESH FRUIT MUESLI

3 dessert apples, cored and chopped or grated
2 bananas, thinly sliced
30 ml (2 tablespoons) lemon juice
180 ml (12 tablespoons) Muesli base (1) or (2) (page 61)

45 ml (3 tablespoons) shredded coconut
3 satsumas or tangerines, peeled and segmented
30 ml (2 tablespoons) pumpkin seeds

Toss the apples and bananas in lemon juice and then mix all
the ingredients together. Fresh fruit muesli is refreshing and
different served with unsweetened fruit juice and topped
with plain yoghurt or soured cream.
Serves 4

* This is a good 'winter mix' of fresh fruits. In summertime,
you'll want to use strawberries, raspberries, sliced peaches,
pears or apricots with the grated apple.

SAVOURY MUESLI

It's different. It's crunchy. And it's very good.

180 ml (12 tablespoons) Muesli base (1) or (2) (page 61)
4 tender stalks celery, thinly sliced
2 large carrots, grated
90 ml (6 tablespoons) small cauliflower florets
30 ml (2 tablespoons) sultanas
30 ml (2 tablespoons) millet seeds

Just mix all the ingredients together and serve with chilled
plain yoghurt or buttermilk. Orange juice is good for a
change, too.
Serves 4

PRUNE GRANOLA

It's sweeter and even crunchier than muesli and, breakfast
apart, goes perfectly with raw or cooked dried fruits.

175 g (6 oz) Muesli base (1) or (2) (page 61)
75 g (3 oz) shredded coconut

50 g (2 oz) chopped hazelnuts
25 g (1 oz) sesame seeds
25 g (1 oz) sunflower seeds
100 g (4 oz) clear honey
45 ml (3 tablespoons) light Muscovado sugar
45 ml (3 tablespoons) oil
175 g (6 oz) pitted prunes, chopped

Mix together the muesli, coconut, nuts and seeds. Melt together the honey, sugar and oil, pour over the dry ingredients and mix thoroughly. Spread on two baking trays and cook in a preheated oven, 160°C (325°F), Gas 3, for 25 minutes, stirring occasionally. Stir in the chopped prunes and leave to cool completely.

Store in an airtight container.

Makes about 750 g (1¼ lb)

* Other dried fruits are good, and often preferred. Try chopped apricots, apple rings, pears or peaches.

PORRIDGE

A first-class fibre start to the day. If you're not too tied to tradition, add more, as you do to muesli, in the form of chopped dried fruits.

100 g (4 oz) medium oatmeal
25 g (1 oz) oatbran and oatgerm
600 ml (1 pint) boiling water
salt

For serving
honey (optional)

Have the water boiling in a pan (a non-stick one is an advantage). Sprinkle on the oat products, stir rapidly and bring back to the boil, still stirring. Lower the heat to

minimum and simmer very gently for 20 minutes, stirring occasionally. Stir in the salt and serve at once, with honey if desired.
Serves 4

HERB-GARDEN RICE

Colour it green, and a rice dish looks and tastes remarkably different. It's good to serve with a medley of steamed vegetables or a crunchy salad.

    225 g (8 oz) brown rice, washed and drained
    600 ml (1 pint) vegetable stock (page 12), or water
    salt
    50 g (2 oz) margarine
    100 g (4 oz) celery, finely chopped
    8 spring onions, peeled and thinly sliced
    75 g (3 oz) fresh chopped mixed herbs, e.g. parsley, mar-
      joram, thyme
    pepper

Cook the rice in the stock or salted water for 30 minutes. Melt the margarine in a pan and stir-fry the celery for 3–4 minutes over moderate heat. Stir the celery, onions and herbs into the rice and season with pepper. Cover the pan and continue cooking for 10–15 minutes, or until the rice is tender.
Serves 4

SPICED RICE

A subtle way to introduce a different spice blend when serving curry.

    seeds from 12 cardamom pods
    6 black peppercorns

12 whole cloves
5 ml (1 teaspoon) fennel seeds
2.5 ml (½ teaspoon) ground turmeric
5 ml (1 teaspoon) salt
5 ml (1 teaspoon) light Muscovado sugar
30 ml (2 tablespoons) oil
2 medium onions, peeled and finely chopped
2 cloves garlic, peeled and crushed
225 g (8 oz) brown rice, washed and drained
600 ml (1 pint) water

For garnish
30 ml (2 tablespoons) chopped fresh coriander leaves, or
  chervil or parsley

Grind the spices and mix them with the turmeric, salt and sugar. Heat the oil in a pan and fry the onion and garlic over moderate heat for 3 minutes, stirring once or twice. Add the spice mixture and stir-fry for 2 minutes. Add the rice and stir for 1 minute then pour on the water. Bring to the boil, cover and simmer for 40–45 minutes or until the rice is just tender. Garnish with the chopped herb.
Serves 4

AMERICAN RICE

Often it is left to the rice dish to provide not only valuable fibre, but colour too. This one does, cheerfully.

45 ml (3 tablespoons) oil
1 medium onion, peeled and thinly sliced
2 cloves garlic, peeled and crushed
10 ml (2 teaspoons) caraway seeds
2.5 ml (½ teaspoon) cumin seeds
225 g (8 oz) brown rice, washed and drained
600 ml (1 pint) vegetable stock (page 12)

30 ml (2 tablespoons) tomato purée
5 ml (1 teaspoon) dried oregano
salt and pepper
450 g (1 lb) tomatoes, skinned and chopped

For garnish
45 ml (3 tablespoons) chopped fresh basil, or parsley

Heat the oil in a pan and fry the onion and garlic over moderate heat for 4–5 minutes, stirring occasionally. Add the caraway and cumin seeds and stir for 1 minute, then put in the rice and stir for a further minute. Add the stock and tomato purée, bring to the boil and season with the dried herb, salt and pepper. Cover the pan and simmer for 40–45 minutes. Stir in the tomatoes and set aside in a warm place for 10 minutes. Serve garnished with the chopped herb.
Serves 4

RAISIN AND PISTACHIO PILAFF

The most delicious partner I've found for this Turkish-style pilaff is – surprisingly – a plain omelette.

45 ml (3 tablespoons) oil
225 g (8 oz) brown rice, washed and drained
600 ml (1 pint) vegetable stock (page 12), or water
salt and pepper
100 g (4 oz) seedless raisins
100 g (4 oz) pistachios, or mixed nuts
4 spring onions, peeled and thinly sliced

Heat the oil in a pan, add the rice and stir-fry over moderate heat for 1 minute. Pour on the stock or water, bring to the boil, cover and lower the heat. Simmer for 35 minutes. Season with salt and pepper. Add the raisins and nuts and stir gently. Cover and simmer for a further 5–10 minutes, or

until the rice is just tender. Stir in the sliced onions. Serve hot.
Serves 4

LENTIL KEDGEREE

A tossed green salad would go perfectly with this medium-spiced pulse and grain dish. So would mango chutney and spiced poppadoms.

60 ml (4 tablespoons) oil
2 medium onions, peeled and finely chopped
3 cloves garlic, peeled and finely chopped
1 green chilli, seeded and finely chopped
5 ml (1 teaspoon) garam masala
5 ml (1 teaspoon) ground cumin
2.5 ml (½ teaspoon) ground turmeric
225 g (8 oz) green or brown lentils, soaked and drained
225 g (8 oz) brown rice, washed and drained
850 ml (1½ pints) vegetable stock (page 12), or water
salt
60 ml (4 tablespoons) sultanas
30 ml (2 tablespoons) chopped fresh coriander, or parsley

For garnish
2 hard-boiled eggs, quartered
2 bananas, sliced
15 ml (1 tablespoon) lemon juice
45 ml (3 tablespoons) desiccated coconut

For the sauce
150 ml (¼ pint) plain yoghurt
30 ml (2 tablespoons) chopped fresh coriander, or mint
pepper

Heat the oil in a pan and fry the onion over moderate heat for 3–4 minutes, stirring once or twice. Add the garlic, chilli and ground spices and stir-fry for 2 minutes. Stir in the lentils and rice. Pour on the stock or water, bring to the boil, cover, lower the heat and simmer for 45 minutes, or until the lentils and rice are just tender. (Check during the cooking and add a little boiling water if needed.) Stir in the salt, sultanas and herb and turn into a heated dish.

Garnish with the egg wedges, the bananas tossed in lemon juice, and the coconut.

For the sauce, stir together the yoghurt and herb and season with pepper. Hand separately.

Serves 6

BAKED VEGETABLE PILAFF

If you are using the oven for another dish, this method might be more convenient than cooking on top of the stove.

40 g (1½ oz) margarine
1 medium onion, peeled and finely chopped
1 clove garlic, peeled and crushed
4 stalks celery, thinly sliced
225 g (8 oz) brown rice, washed and drained
100 g (4 oz) button mushrooms, sliced
2 medium carrots, finely diced
600 ml (1 pint) vegetable stock (page 12)
salt and pepper
50 g (2 oz) seedless raisins
50 g (2 oz) pecan halves

Melt the margarine in a flameproof casserole and fry the onion, garlic and celery over moderate heat for 3-4 minutes, stirring occasionally. Stir in the rice to coat the grains thoroughly, then the mushrooms and carrots. Pour on the stock, bring to the boil and cover the dish.

Cook in a preheated oven, 180°C (350°F), Gas 4, for 35 minutes. Season with salt and pepper, stir in the raisins,

cover again and cook for a further 10 minutes. Stir in the pecans and leave in a warm place to 'rest' for 10 minutes, before serving.
Serves 4

VEGETABLE PAELLA

A planned-ahead dish that uses cooked rice and vegetables.

    25 g (1 oz) margarine
    30 ml (2 tablespoons) oil
    2 medium onions, peeled and chopped
    2 cloves garlic, peeled and crushed
    100 g (4 oz) mushrooms, sliced
    225 g (8 oz) cooked carrots, diced
    175 g (6 oz) canned sweetcorn, drained
    100 g (4 oz) cooked peas
    225 g (8 oz) cooked brown rice
    45 ml (3 tablespoons) sunflower seeds
    salt and pepper
    15 ml (1 tablespoon) soy sauce
    3 eggs

Heat the margarine and oil in a pan and fry the onion and garlic over moderate heat for 3–4 minutes, stirring occasionally. Add the mushrooms and cook for 2 minutes, then add the carrots, sweetcorn and peas. Stir to mix the vegetables evenly. Stir in the rice and sunflower seeds and season with salt, pepper and soy sauce. Cook, stirring often, until all the ingredients are heated through. Just before serving, stir in the whole eggs.

Serve with grated cheese and Tomato Sauce (page 261) or Mushroom Sauce (page 262).
Serves 4

RICE SALAD RING

A moulded rice ring makes a perfect container for other salads – courgettes in curry dressing, for example, or sliced apples with an orange and yoghurt dressing.

150 g (5 oz) brown rice, washed and drained
375 ml (13 fl oz) water
salt
30 ml (2 tablespoons) oil
1 medium onion, peeled and chopped
2 cloves garlic, peeled and crushed
1 green pepper, seeded and chopped
1 red pepper, seeded and chopped
½ small cucumber, finely diced
50 g (2 oz) button mushrooms, chopped
30 ml (2 tablespoons) sunflower seeds

For the dressing
60 ml (4 tablespoons) vinaigrette dressing (page 54)
a pinch of paprika
75 ml (3 tablespoons) chopped fresh mint, or parsley

For garnish
4 large tomatoes, quartered

Put the rice into a pan with the water and salt, bring to the boil, stir and cover. Lower the heat and simmer for 40–45 minutes, or until the rice is tender and has absorbed the water.

While the rice is cooking, heat the oil in a pan and fry the onion and garlic over moderate heat, stirring occasionally, for 4 minutes. Stir in the peppers, cucumber, mushrooms, sunflower seeds and remove from the heat.

Mix together the dressing, paprika and herb. To assemble the dish, stir together the onion mixture, vegetables, rice and dressing. Press the resultant salad into a greased 850-ml (1½-

pint) ring mould and level the top. Allow to cool, then chill in the refrigerator for about 1 hour.

Unmould the salad on to a serving plate and surround it with the tomato wedges. Fill the centre with a contrasting salad of your choice.

Serves 4

CHEESE RICE CAKES

175 g (6 oz) brown rice, washed and drained
salt
425 ml (¾ pint) water
175 g (6 oz) cheese, grated
30 ml (2 tablespoons) grated Parmesan cheese
60 ml (4 tablespoons) ground almonds
30 ml (2 tablespoons) chopped fresh parsley or mint
salt and pepper
1 egg, beaten
about 75 ml (3 tablespoons) crushed bran crispbread

Simmer the rice in the salted water for 40–45 minutes, or until it is just tender. While it is still hot, mix the rice with the cheeses, almonds and herb and season with salt and pepper. Leave the mixture to cool.

Shape the mixture into 8 round cakes. Dip each one in the egg mixture and then coat them with the crumbs. Place the rice cakes on a greased baking tray and cook in a pre-heated oven, 200°C (400°F), Gas 6, for 20–25 minutes, turning them once.

Serve hot, with Tomato Sauce (page 261) or Mushroom Sauce (page 262) and a salad.

Serves 4

GNOCCHI

A substantial main dish in their own right or an accompaniment to a lighter one, these semolina cakes are agreeably versatile.

600 ml (1 pint) milk
1 bay leaf
150 g (5 oz) wholewheat semolina
3 eggs
175 g (6 oz) cheese, grated
salt and pepper
a pinch of grated nutmeg
a pinch of cayenne pepper
45 ml (3 tablespoons) milk
about 90 ml (6 tablespoons) crushed bran crispbread
30 ml (2 tablespoons) millet seeds
fat for shallow frying

Bring the milk to the boil with the bay leaf. Leave to infuse for 5 minutes then discard the leaf. Boil the milk again and tip in the semolina, stirring vigorously. Reduce the heat to low and stir continuously until the mixture thickens. Remove from the heat.

Beat 2 of the eggs and stir them with the cheese into the mixture. Season with salt, pepper, nutmeg and cayenne. Grease a Swiss roll tin, spread the mixture evenly over it and set aside to cool. When it is quite cold, cut into 4-cm (1½-in) squares.

Beat the remaining eggs with the milk. Stir together the crispbread crumbs and millet seeds. Dip each piece of gnocchi first into the egg, then into the crumbs to coat each square on both sides.

Fry the squares in shallow fat to brown them on both sides. Serve the Tomato sauce (page 261) or Cheese sauce (page 100) and salad. Alternatively serve them as an accompaniment to a main dish such as filled vegetables. *Serves 6*

* Instead of coating the gnocchi with egg and crumbs, you can arrange them in an ovenproof dish, cover them with Cheese sauce (page 100) and tomato slices and brown for 5 minutes under a hot grill. Serve with salad.

TABBOULEH

A Lebanese salad in which the cracked wheat supports a tasty mixture of herbs and vegetables.

    225 g (8 oz) burghul (cracked wheat)
    4 spring onions, peeled and finely chopped
    75 ml (5 tablespoons) chopped fresh parsley
    75 ml (5 tablespoons) chopped fresh mint
    4 medium tomatoes, skinned and chopped
    60 ml (4 tablespoons) olive oil
    60 ml (4 tablespoons) lemon juice
    salt and pepper
    about 18 young spinach leaves, shredded

    For garnish
    black olives

    For serving
    wholewheat pitta bread

Soak the wheat in water for 1 hour. Drain well. Pile it into the centre of a clean tea towel, fold over the cloth to enclose the wheat and twist each end in opposite directions. Wring out the cloth to remove all moisture from the wheat.

In a bowl, mix the wheat with the onions, herbs, tomatoes, oil and lemon juice and season well with salt and pepper.

Line a dish with the shredded spinach, pile the wheat

salad into the centre and garnish it with the olives. Serve with fingers of hot pitta bread.
Serves 6

* 'Dipsticks' of raw vegetables make marvellous accompaniments. Choose from spring onions, celery, carrots, peppers and others (see page 52).

BAZARGAN

A Middle-Eastern salad of cracked wheat and walnuts. Serve it as a first course, or with lots of green salad to make a light lunch dish.

175 g (6 oz) burghul (cracked wheat)
4 spring onions, peeled and finely chopped
45 ml (3 tablespoons) tomato purée
30 ml (2 tablespoons) chopped fresh parsley
15 ml (1 tablespoon) chopped fresh oregano, or marjoram
   (or use 5 ml (1 teaspoon) dried herb)
45 ml (3 tablespoons) olive oil
50 g (2 oz) walnuts, chopped
2.5 ml (½ teaspoon) ground allspice
2.5 ml (½ teaspoon) ground cumin
a pinch of cayenne pepper
salt

Soak, drain and dry the wheat as described in the previous recipe. Place the wheat in a bowl and mix in all the other ingredients. Taste a little and add more seasoning if needed – it should be spicy. Cover and leave in the refrigerator overnight. Remove the salad from the fridge and set aside at room temperature for about 1 hour before serving.
Serves 6

BURGHUL PILAFF

You can add extra flavours and colours of your choice – more fibre too – by stirring in a variety of cooked vegetables, nuts or dried fruits.

    30 ml (2 tablespoons) oil
    1 large onion, peeled and finely chopped
    450 ml (16 fl oz) vegetable stock (page 12)
    225 g (8 oz) burghul (cracked wheat), washed and drained
    salt
    75 g (3 oz) dried apricots, chopped
    50 g (2 oz) dried stoned dates, chopped

Heat the oil in a large pan and fry the onion over moderate heat for 4–5 minutes, stirring occasionally. Pour on the stock, bring to the boil and tip in the burghul. Stir well, cover the pan and simmer for 20 minutes, stirring from time to time. Taste and add salt if necessary. Mix in the apricots and dates. Serve hot.
Serves 4

WHOLEWHEAT SALAD

Rice salads there are in abundance. This one, with a light curry dressing, hopefully makes a welcome change.

    225 g (8 oz) wholewheat, soaked overnight and drained
    salt
    1 green pepper, seeded and thinly sliced
    2 canned pimentos, drained and thinly sliced
    4 spring onions, peeled and thinly sliced
    60 ml (4 tablespoons) seedless raisins
    60 ml (4 tablespoons) cashew nuts
    30 ml (2 tablespoons) chopped fresh parsley
    15 ml (1 tablespoon) chopped chives

For the dressing
5 ml (1 teaspoon) curry powder
5 ml (1 teaspoon) light Muscovado sugar
1 clove garlic, peeled and crushed
120 ml (8 tablespoons) Vinaigrette dressing (page 54)

For serving
endive or other salad leaves

Cook the wheat in a large pan of boiling, salted water for
1¼–1½ hours, until the grains begin to split. Drain.

Prepare the dressing by mixing together the curry
powder, sugar and garlic and stirring in the dressing. Pour
this mixture over the wheat while it is still hot, then leave
to cool.

Stir in the remaining ingredients. Pile the salad on to a
dish lined with endive or other salad leaves.
Serves 4

MILLET PILAFF

With a green salad, this is a meal in itself, full of texture and
colour.

225 g (8 oz) millet seeds, washed and drained
salt
700 ml (1¼ pints) vegetable stock (page 12)
225 g (8 oz) cauliflower florets
30 ml (2 tablespoons) oil
1 large onion, peeled and thinly sliced
2 leeks, well washed and sliced
2 medium courgettes, thinly sliced
30 ml (2 tablespoons) chopped chives
pepper
50 g (2 oz) sultanas

For the sauce
150 ml (¼ pint) plain yoghurt
5 ml (1 teaspoon) curry paste
15 ml (1 tablespoon) chopped fresh mint
a few drops of lemon juice

Put the millet and salt into a pan with the stock, bring to the boil, cover and simmer for about 30 minutes, stirring occasionally, until the grain is just tender and the liquid absorbed.

Steam or boil the cauliflower for 5 minutes, drain and refresh in cold water to prevent further cooking. Drain again.

Heat the oil in a pan and fry the onion and leeks over moderate heat for 3 minutes, stirring occasionally; add the courgettes and cook for a further 3 minutes. Stir in the chives and season with pepper and salt if needed.

Stir the vegetable mixture and the sultanas into the millet and set aside to 'rest' in a warm place for 4–5 minutes, then serve.

Mix together the sauce ingredients and serve separately.
Serves 4

MILLET WITH CHEESE

A light and fluffy accompaniment to a main dish. Especially good with filled vegetables or tomato-based gratins.

100 g (4 oz) millet seeds
350 ml (13 fl oz) vegetable stock (page 12)
5 ml (1 teaspoon) yeast extract
salt and pepper
50 g (2 oz) cheese, grated
50 g (2 oz) cheese, cubed

For garnish
30 ml (2 tablespoons) chopped fresh parsley

Put the millet into a pan with the stock and yeast extract. Stir well, bring to the boil and cover the pan. Simmer for about 30 minutes, stirring occasionally, or until the grain is just tender. Season with salt and pepper and stir in the grated cheese. Stir over low heat until the cheese melts. Stir in the cheese cubes. Serve very hot, garnished with the parsley.

Serves 4

CARROT AND OAT CAKE

A main dish that couldn't be simpler – or more delicious. Fresh green vegetables such as broccoli spears and spinach make a good accompaniment.

150 g (5 oz) rolled porridge oats
25 g (1 oz) coarse oatmeal
175 g (6 oz) cheese, grated
175 g (6 oz) carrots, grated
30 ml (2 tablespoons) chopped fresh mint
salt and pepper
1 egg, beaten
50 g (2 oz) margarine, melted
2 tomatoes, thinly sliced
5 ml (1 teaspoon) mixed dried herbs

For the sauce
25 g (1 oz) margarine
15 ml (1 tablespoon) wholewheat flour
275 ml (½ pint) milk
30 ml (2 tablespoons) chopped fresh parsley
5 ml (1 teaspoon) cider vinegar

Mix together in a bowl the oats, oatmeal, cheese, carrots and mint and season with salt and pepper. Beat in the egg. Reserve 15 ml (1 tablespoon) of the melted margarine and stir the remainder into the oat mixture. Turn the mixture into a greased baking tin 23 × 18 cm (9 × 7 in) and level the top. Decorate with the tomato slices and sprinkle over the herbs and reserved margarine. Bake in a pre-heated oven, 190°C (375°F), Gas 5, for 30 minutes, until the cake is golden brown.

Meanwhile make the sauce. Melt the margarine in a pan, stir in the flour and gradually pour on the milk, stirring continuously. Simmer for 5 minutes. Stir in the parsley and vinegar and season with salt and pepper.

Serve the cake hot, handing the sauce separately.

Serves 4

OAT AND VEGETABLE CASSEROLE

This main dish is sharply flavoured but bland in colour. A green vegetable such as broccoli or spinach makes a good accompaniment.

    1 medium cauliflower, cut into florets
    2 small white turnips, finely diced
    2 medium carrots, finely diced
    salt
    50 g (2 oz) margarine
    30 ml (2 tablespoons) wholewheat flour
    150 ml (¼ pint) milk
    150 ml (¼ pint) plain yoghurt
    pepper
    5 ml (1 teaspoon) Meaux mustard
    100 g (4 oz) cheese, grated
    45 ml (3 tablespoons) chopped fresh parsley
    150 g (5 oz) rolled porridge oats
    50 g (2 oz) chopped walnuts

Steam the cauliflower, turnips and carrots over salted water for 10 minutes. Refresh them in cold water to prevent further cooking, then drain.

Melt half the margarine in a small pan, stir in the flour and cook to form a roux. Gradually pour on the milk, stirring continuously. When the mixture thickens, pour in the yoghurt and stir until the sauce has blended. Season with salt, pepper and the mustard and simmer for 3 minutes. Stir in half the cheese, and the parsley.

Turn the vegetables into a shallow ovenproof dish, pour on the sauce and stir with a fork to mix well. Melt the remaining margarine, stir in the oats, walnuts and remaining cheese and spread over the vegetables. Bake in a pre-heated oven, 200°C (400°F), Gas 6, for 30 minutes, until the top is golden brown.
Serves 4

BARLEY AND BEAN CASSEROLE

Slow-cook the grains and pulses, then add your selection of seasonal vegetables towards the end.

   50 g (2 oz) margarine
   1 large onion, peeled and sliced
   2 cloves garlic, peeled and finely chopped
   100 g (4 oz) pot barley, washed and drained
   375 g (12 oz) dried white haricot beans, soaked overnight
      and drained
   1.1 litres (2 pints) vegetable stock (page 12)
   10 ml (2 teaspoons) yeast extract
   2 bay leaves
   1 bouquet garni
   2 large carrots, diced
   2 small white turnips, diced
   2 medium courgettes, sliced

   100 g (4 oz) button mushrooms, sliced if large
   salt and pepper
   45 ml (3 tablespoons) chopped fresh parsley
   60 ml (4 tablespoons) wholewheat breadcrumbs

Melt half the margarine in a flameproof casserole and fry the
onion and garlic over moderate heat for 5 minutes, stirring
occasionally. Add the barley, beans, stock, yeast extract, bay
leaves and bouquet garni, stir well and bring to the boil.
Cover and cook in a pre-heated oven, 150°C (300°F), Gas 2,
for 2 hours.

   Stir in the carrots and turnips and cook for a further 30
minutes, adding a little more stock if necessary. Meanwhile,
melt the remaining margarine in a pan and fry the
courgettes and mushrooms for 5 minutes, then stir them into
the casserole. Discard the bay leaves and bouquet garni,
season with salt and pepper and stir in the parsley. Sprinkle
the breadcrumbs on top and return the casserole to the oven
for 30 minutes.

   Serve with lots of hot, fresh wholewheat bread and
perhaps a green salad.
Serves 6

4 Pasta

How could pasta possibly be more versatile? Or simple to prepare? Or more maligned? It couldn't. Choose wholewheat pasta and you are well on the way to your fibre-intake target, the deliciously easy way.

In all its various shapes and sizes, wholewheat pasta can be served as a simple accompaniment to a main vegetable dish; tossed perhaps just with butter and fresh herbs, with cream or – my own pet way – soured cream. As the following recipes show, pasta partners lovely vegetable sauces and vegetable medleys for main dishes with endless variety – mushroom and walnut; spinach and cottage cheese; French bean and cauliflower; lentil, garlic and tomato. When time's short, it's a quick toss-up: the pasta and the sauce together; a salad and a dressing – and there's a substantial meal.

Wholewheat pasta has a role in lovely layered dishes too: lasagne with courgette and tomato sauce and a cheesy topping; macaroni baked with spinach and cheese; short-cut macaroni with rich red lentil sauce in the Greek country style – these are all perfect supper, even party, dishes that can be completely prepared in advance, just ready for baking.

As some of these dishes involve cooked wholewheat pasta it makes time-and-motion-study sense to cook twice as much as you need for one meal and so have some ready for another. Drained and cooled, pasta stores well for 2–3 days in a covered container in the refrigerator. Cook extra for salads, too: toss the pasta in French dressing (pages 54-5) while it's still hot, leave it to cool and it's ready to be mixed with the vegetables, fruits and nuts of your choice.

Dietary fibre

Over the years, poor old pasta has acquired a bad name for 'being fattening' and been utterly shunned by many weight-conscious people, which is a pity. Left to its own devices – without all the calorie-packed sauces and stuffings we enjoy – it is full of nutrients and not so full of calories.

Anyone wishing to make a gradual change to a diet that includes more fibre can make great strides, just by switching to wholewheat pasta. This is the rich brown kind with the wholesome look and a nutty flavour, made from whole durum wheat.

Wholewheat pasta has a dietary fibre content of at least 10 per cent of the dry weight and, for the record, contains 2.8 per cent fat and 65.7 per cent starch.

Cooking

At present wholewheat pasta is available in a limited, though increasing variety of shapes which are all quick to cook. Tagliatelle, long noodle ribbons, takes 9 minutes; short-cut macaroni, 10 minutes; rings, 12 minutes; large shells, 12 minutes; spaghetti, 12-14 minutes; lasagne, 16 minutes. But there is now – good news – a 'no pre-cook' type of wholewheat lasagne that softens and swells in the sauce as it is baked. Allow an extra 25 per cent liquid in the sauce when using this type.

To cook wholewheat pasta, drop it gradually into a large pan of boiling, salted water, stir well to separate the pieces and bring the water quickly back to the boil. Partly cover the pan, with the lid tilted, and boil gently for 9-14 minutes, or according to the directions on the packet, until it is just tender. Don't overcook it, or it will lose both texture and flavour.

Drain the pasta in a colander and then, if you wish, run it under hot water to wash off any remaining starch and to further separate the pieces. Drain well (give shell shapes a vigorous tossing, to get rid of water trapped in the hollows). If your self-set fat allowance permits, toss all pasta to be served without a sauce in plain butter, or a herb-flavoured one such as parsley, mint or garlic butter (page 264). Here's one instance where, if it's flavour that counts, butter really is preferable to other fats.

Lasagne verde and other spinach-added green pastas make a very enjoyable alternative to wholewheat kinds. They are made, though, from *refined* durum wheat, and are therefore appreciably lower in fibre. Choose them perhaps when you plan a maxi-fibre sauce, such as one with lentils, to provide a contrast of flavour and colour.

TAGLIATELLE WITH MUSHROOM SAUCE

The pasta's filling, the sauce is good and rich. All you need as an accompaniment is a cool, green salad.

350 g (12 oz) wholewheat tagliatelle, or other pasta shapes
salt

For the sauce
50 g (2 oz) margarine, or butter
2 cloves garlic, peeled and crushed
175 g (6 oz) button mushrooms, sliced
225 g (8 oz) cream cheese
60 ml (4 tablespoons) chopped chives
salt and pepper
60 ml (4 tablespoons) chopped walnuts

Cook the pasta in boiling, salted water for 9 minutes or until it is just tender.

While the pasta's cooking, there's plenty of time to make the sauce. Melt the fat in a pan and fry the garlic and mushrooms, stirring now and again, over moderate heat for about 3 minutes. Stir in the cream cheese and half the chives, season with salt and pepper and allow the cheese just to melt. Stir in the walnuts.

Pour the sauce over the pasta, toss well, and garnish with the reserved chives.

Serves 4

MACARONI WITH LEGUMES SAUCE

Here's a fibre-feast, appropriate for highdays and holidays.

225 g (8 oz) short-cut wholewheat macaroni, or other pasta shapes
salt
225 g (8 oz) French beans, trimmed and sliced
1 small cauliflower, cut into florets

For the sauce
60 ml (4 tablespoons) olive oil
2 cloves garlic, peeled and crushed
2 medium courgettes, thinly sliced
100 g (4 oz) button mushrooms, sliced
100 g (4 oz) frozen peas, thawed
30 ml (2 tablespoons) chopped fresh parsley
5 ml (1 teaspoon) dried oregano
pepper

For serving
grated Parmesan cheese

Cook the macaroni in boiling, salted water for 10 minutes, or until it is just tender. Drain. At the same time, steam the beans and cauliflower or cook them in boiling, salted water for 4-5 minutes. Drain and plunge them into cold water to prevent further cooking, then drain again.

Heat the oil in a pan and fry the garlic, courgettes and mushrooms over moderate heat, stirring almost constantly, for 3 minutes. Stir in the peas, cauliflower, beans, parsley and oregano. Season with pepper and cook for 2 minutes more.

Toss the pasta and sauce together and serve at once, with the cheese handed separately.

Serves 4

WEDDING-RING SPINACH

The pasta rings are piled on a bed of creamy spinach, and it's very, very tasty.

900 g (2 lb) spinach
salt
225 g (8 oz) wholewheat pasta rings
50 g (2 oz) butter
1 medium onion, peeled and finely chopped
1 clove garlic, peeled and crushed
225 g (8 oz) cream cheese
15 ml (1 tablespoon) lemon juice
pepper
45 ml (3 tablespoons) walnut halves

Wash the spinach and discard the tough stalks. Cook it in plenty of boiling, salted water for 8-10 minutes, until the leaves are just tender. Drain into a colander and press well against the sides to extract all the moisture. Chop the spinach very finely.

Meanwhile, cook the pasta in boiling, salted water for 12 minutes, or until it is just tender. Drain.

Melt half the butter in a pan and fry the onion and garlic

over moderate heat for 4–5 minutes, stirring occasionally. Stir in the spinach, cream cheese and lemon juice and season well with salt and pepper. Heat through thoroughly. Turn the spinach mixture on to a heated serving dish. Toss the remaining butter and the walnuts with the pasta rings. Arrange them on the spinach and serve at once.
Serves 4

PASTA WITH PESTO

When fresh basil is in season, you can sometimes buy it in the markets and, with this sauce, remind yourself of Italy or Greece. Sorry, but dried basil won't do.

350 g (12 oz) wholewheat tagliatelle, or other pasta shapes
salt
50 g (2 oz) butter

For the pesto sauce
90 ml (6 tablespoons) olive oil
4 cloves garlic, peeled
50 g (2 oz) fresh basil leaves
75 g (3 oz) pine nuts
75 g (3 oz) Parmesan cheese, grated
pepper

Cook the pasta in boiling, salted water for 9 minutes, or until it is just tender. Drain.

In a blender, make a nice green sauce by whizzing the oil, garlic, basil and nuts. Stir in the cheese and season the sauce with salt and pepper.

Toss the pasta with the butter and then with the pesto sauce.
Serves 4

* Use this sauce with the following recipe, too.

VEGETABLES WITH PESTO SAUCE

The aromatic basil and cheese sauce is used for a traditional Italian dish that's an appetizing cream-and-greeny combination.

1 recipe Pesto sauce (see previous recipe)
225 g (8 oz) potatoes, scrubbed and thickly diced
225 g (8 oz) French beans, trimmed
salt
175 g (6 oz) wholewheat tagliatelle, or other pasta shapes
freshly ground black pepper

Make the sauce as described.

Cook the potatoes and beans in boiling, salted water or by steaming until they are only just tender. Cook the pasta in boiling, salted water for 9 minutes, or until it is just tender. Drain the vegetables and the pasta, mix them together, grind on black pepper and straightaway pour the sauce over them. Serve at once.
Serves 4

MACARONI WITH RIBBON SAUCE

The 'ribbons' are the strips of green, red and (if you can get them) yellow peppers that brighten up a dull day.

275 g (10 oz) short-cut wholewheat macaroni, or other pasta shapes
salt

For the sauce
45 ml (3 tablespoons) olive oil
2 large onions, peeled and chopped
1 medium head fennel, very thinly sliced (or use 4 stalks celery)
2 cloves garlic, peeled and crushed

1 green pepper, seeded and thinly sliced
1 red pepper, seeded and thinly sliced
1 yellow pepper, seeded and thinly sliced (or use another
    green or red one)
450 g (1 lb) tomatoes, skinned and sliced
10 ml (2 teaspoons) dried oregano
salt and pepper

To make the sauce, heat the oil in a pan and fry the onions, fennel and garlic over moderate heat, stirring often, for 4 minutes. Add all the peppers and cook for a further 2 minutes, stirring occasionally. Add the tomatoes and oregano and season well with salt and pepper. Simmer gently, the pan uncovered, for 5 minutes, until the vegetables are tender.

Meanwhile, cook the pasta in boiling, salted water for 10 minutes, or until it is just tender, then drain.

Toss the macaroni and the sauce together and leave to stand in a warm place for 2–3 minutes before serving.
Serves 4

PASTA AND PEAS

At the height of summer, this is a great way to use fresh peas. Other times? Well, frozen ones will do.

275 g (10 oz) wholewheat spaghetti, or other long-shape
    pasta
salt
450 g (1 lb) fresh peas, shelled
5 ml (1 teaspoon) light Muscovado sugar
75 g (3 oz) butter
30 ml (2 tablespoons) chopped fresh mint
90 ml (6 tablespoons) grated Parmesan cheese
pepper, freshly ground

Cook the spaghetti in boiling, salted water for 12-14 minutes, or until it is just tender. Drain.

Meanwhile, cook the peas in a little boiling, salted water with the sugar for 8 minutes, or until they are barely tender. Drain and toss them in half the butter and all the mint. Stir the remaining butter and the cheese into the pasta, add the peas and as much pepper as you have the patience to grind. Toss well and serve at once.

Serves 4

SPAGHETTI WITH AUBERGINE SAUCE

It's a wine-red sauce, rich and dark – and rather exotic. A green salad goes well with this dish.

350 g (12 oz) wholewheat spaghetti, or other pasta shapes
salt

For the sauce
30 ml (2 tablespoons) oil
25 g (1 oz) butter
2 medium onions, peeled and thinly sliced
2 cloves garlic, peeled and finely chopped
1 small aubergine, finely diced
225 g (8 oz) tomatoes, peeled and chopped
10 ml (2 teaspoons) dried oregano
15 ml (1 tablespoon) chopped fresh parsley
salt and pepper
60 ml (4 tablespoons) red wine

For serving
grated Parmesan cheese

To make the sauce, heat the oil and butter in a pan and fry the onions and garlic over moderate heat for 2 minutes, stirring once or twice. Add the aubergine and cook for a further 2 minutes, then stir in the tomatoes and herbs. Season with salt and pepper, bring to the boil, cover and simmer for 30 minutes. Stir the wine into the sauce, taste and adjust the seasoning. Bring to the boil and simmer for 10 minutes.

Meanwhile cook the spaghetti in boiling, salted water for 12–14 minutes, or until it is just tender. Drain.

Toss the pasta and sauce together and serve, with the cheese handed separately.

Serves 4

SPAGHETTI WITH SOURED CREAM

When the pasta is being served as an accompaniment – to a trug-ful of steamed garden vegetables perhaps – it couldn't be more delicious.

275 g (10 oz) wholewheat spaghetti, or other pasta shapes
salt
25 g (1 oz) butter
1 medium onion, peeled and finely chopped
1 clove garlic, peeled and finely chopped
15 ml (1 tablespoon) wholewheat flour
300 ml (½ pint) soured cream
30 ml (2 tablespoons) chopped fresh parsley
pepper

For serving
grated Parmesan cheese

Cook the spaghetti in boiling, salted water for 12–14 minutes, or until it is just tender. Drain.

Melt the butter in a pan and fry the onion and garlic over moderate heat for 4–5 minutes, stirring often. Stir in the flour and cook for a further 2 minutes. Beat in the soured cream and just heat through. Stir in the parsley and season

with salt and pepper. Toss the pasta with the sauce and hand
the cheese separately.
Serves 4

LASAGNE WITH COURGETTE SAUCE

When you are well in credit with high-fibre wholewheat
pasta, you can afford to combine it with some low-fibre
ingredients – like courgettes – which provide a good texture
and flavour contrast.

175 g (6 oz) wholewheat 'no pre-cook' lasagne sheets

For the courgette sauce
45 ml (3 tablespoons) oil
1 medium onion, peeled and thinly sliced
1 clove garlic, peeled and finely chopped
450 g (1 lb) courgettes, thinly sliced
450 g (1 lb) tomatoes, skinned and sliced
30 ml (2 tablespoons) chopped fresh mint
salt and pepper
90 ml (6 tablespoons) dry white wine
60 ml (4 tablespoons) chopped walnuts

For the cheese sauce
25 g (1 oz) margarine
30 ml (2 tablespoons) wholewheat flour
300 ml (½ pint) milk
a pinch of grated nutmeg
salt and pepper
50 g (2 oz) cheese, grated

To make the courgette sauce, first heat the oil in a pan and
fry the onion and garlic over moderate heat for 3 minutes,
stirring once or twice. Add the courgettes and cook for a
further 4 minutes, stirring often. Add the tomatoes, mint,

salt and pepper. Bring the sauce to the boil and simmer very gently for 20 minutes. Add the wine and walnuts, bring to the boil and simmer slowly for a further 10 minutes. Taste and adjust the seasoning if needed. Set aside.

To make the cheese sauce, melt the margarine in a pan, stir in the flour and gradually pour on the milk. Bring to the boil, stirring, and simmer for 3 minutes. Season with nutmeg, salt and pepper and stir in the cheese. Set aside.

Make a layer of lasagne in a shallow baking dish and cover with courgette sauce. Continue to make alternate layers, finishing with courgette sauce. Cover the whole with the cheese sauce. Bake in a pre-heated oven, 190°C (375°F), Gas 5, for 40 minutes, or until the topping is deep brown. Serve very hot.

Serves 4

LENTIL LASAGNE

Good vegetarian dishes never imitate meat ones. This isn't meant to, but the thick lentil sauce does remind some people of the Italian version.

175 g (6 oz) wholewheat 'no pre-cook' lasagne sheets

For the lentil sauce
225 g (8 oz) brown lentils, washed and drained
a bunch of parsley stalks
2 bay leaves
600 ml (1 pint) water
75 ml (5 tablespoons) oil
1 large onion, peeled and thinly sliced
2 cloves garlic, peeled and finely chopped
6 stalks celery, thinly sliced
1 green pepper, seeded and thinly sliced
2 large carrots, grated

2 large tomatoes, skinned and sliced
30 ml (2 tablespoons) tomato purée
750 ml (1¼ pints) vegetable stock (page 12)
10 ml (2 teaspoons) dried oregano
salt and pepper

For the cheese sauce
25 g (1 oz) margarine
15 ml (1 tablespoon) wholewheat flour
150 ml (¼ pint) milk
150 ml (¼ pint) plain yoghurt
2 eggs, beaten
75 g (3 oz) cheese, grated
salt and pepper

Simmer the lentils with the parsley and bay leaves in the water for 50 minutes, or until they are tender but not mushy. Discard the herbs and drain off any water that has not been absorbed.

While the lentils are cooking, heat the oil in a pan and fry the onion, garlic, celery and pepper over moderate heat, stirring often, for 5 minutes. Add the carrots and tomatoes and cook, stirring, for 1 minute. Stir in the tomato purée and stock and bring to the boil. Season with the oregano, salt and pepper, cover and simmer for 30 minutes. Remove from the heat and stir in the lentils. Taste the sauce and add more seasoning if necessary.

To make the cheese sauce, melt the margarine in a pan and stir in the flour, then gradually pour on the milk. Stir until it boils and thickens. Remove from the heat and beat in the yoghurt, eggs and cheese. Season with salt and pepper.

Cover the base of a shallow, well-greased baking dish with lasagne, then add a layer of lentil sauce. Continue to make alternate layers, finishing with lentil sauce. Pour on the cheese sauce.

Bake in a pre-heated oven, 200°C (400°F), Gas 6, for 35–40 minutes, until the topping is well risen and dark brown in colour. Serve very hot.

* If you use wholewheat lasagne that *does* require pre-cooking, reduce the amount of stock in the sauce to 600 ml (1 pint). The 'no pre-cook' type absorbs about 25 per cent of the liquid.

* This lentil sauce, made with 600 ml (1 pint) stock, can be served with wholewheat spaghetti or macaroni. Cook the pasta as usual, toss it with the sauce and sprinkle with grated Parmesan cheese.

* For a change, use the delicious green spinach 'no pre-cook' pasta, lasagne verde.

SPINACH AND CHEESE LASAGNE

A baked pasta 'sandwich', with lasagne and tomato sauce layers enclosing a creamy spinach filling.

175 g (6 oz) wholewheat 'no pre-cook' lasagne sheets

For the sauce
45 ml (3 tablespoons) oil
1 large onion, peeled and thinly sliced
2 cloves garlic, peeled and crushed
4 stalks celery, thinly sliced
850-g (1 lb 14-oz) can tomatoes
5 ml (1 teaspoon) dried oregano
15 ml (1 tablespoon) chopped fresh parsley
2 bay leaves
10 ml (2 teaspoons) dark Muscovado sugar
salt and pepper

For the filling
450 g (1 lb) spinach
350 g (12 oz) cottage cheese
100 g (4 oz) cheese, grated
2 eggs, beaten
a pinch of grated nutmeg
salt and pepper

For the topping
50 g (2 oz) wholewheat breadcrumbs
30 ml (2 tablespoons) sunflower seeds
50 g (2 oz) cheese, grated

To make the sauce, heat the oil in a pan and fry the onion, garlic and celery over moderate heat for 4 minutes, stirring once or twice. Add the tomatoes, herbs and sugar and season with salt and pepper. Bring the sauce to the boil, lower the heat and simmer for 25 minutes. (If you use lasagne that *does* need pre-cooking, simmer the sauce for 40 minutes, to reduce it further.) Discard the bay leaves, taste the sauce and add more sugar or seasoning if needed.

To make the filling, wash the spinach, strip off the stalks and cook the leaves in plenty of boiling salted water for 8–10 minutes. Drain thoroughly, pressing the spinach against the colander to force out all the moisture. Chop finely and leave to cool. Mix the spinach with the cheeses and the beaten eggs and season well with nutmeg, salt and pepper.

Pour one half of the tomato sauce into a greased ovenproof dish, cover with half the lasagne and then with the spinach filling. Cover with the remaining lasagne and then the rest of the sauce. Sprinkle with the breadcrumbs, seeds and grated cheese mixed together. Bake in a pre-heated oven, 190°C (375°F), Gas 5, for 40 minutes. Serve very hot.
Serves 6

BAKED MACARONI WITH SPINACH

An up-dated version of macaroni cheese – up-lifted in fibre, too.

150 g (5 oz) wholewheat macaroni
salt
450 g (1 lb) spinach
50 g (2 oz) margarine
25 g (1 oz) wholewheat flour
600 ml (1 pint) milk (buttermilk is better)
100 g (4 oz) cheese, grated
100 g (4 oz) cottage cheese
a pinch of grated nutmeg
pepper
90 ml (6 tablespoons) wholewheat breadcrumbs

Cook the macaroni in boiling, salted water for 10 minutes, or until it is just tender. Drain.

Wash the spinach, strip off the leaves and cook the leaves in boiling, salted water for 8–10 minutes. Drain the spinach and chop it finely.

Melt the margarine in a pan and stir in the flour. When it forms a roux, gradually pour on the milk or buttermilk, stirring until it boils. Simmer for 3 minutes. Beat half the grated cheese and all the cottage cheese into the sauce and season with nutmeg, salt and pepper. Stir in the spinach and mix very thoroughly.

Pour half the sauce into a well-greased baking dish. Cover with the macaroni and then the remaining sauce. Mix together the reserved cheese and the breadcrumbs and sprinkle over the top.

Bake in a pre-heated oven, 190°C (375°F), Gas 5, for 40 minutes, until the top is dark brown and deliciously crispy.
Serves 4

* As a variation, you can use half the spinach and cheese sauce to fill large, cooked wholewheat pasta shells. Arrange them in a greased baking dish, cover with the remaining sauce (or an ordinary cheese sauce) and the crumb topping and bake as described.

PASTITIO

This is one of my favourite informal supper-party dishes. It can be made a day or two in advance of cooking, and also freezes perfectly. So you can easily divide this larger quantity (which serves 8) in half, on the one-for-now/one-for-later principle.

450 g (1 lb) short-cut wholewheat macaroni
salt
50 g (2 oz) Parmesan cheese, grated

For the lentil sauce
175 g (6 oz) brown lentils, washed and drained
450 ml (¾ pint) water
a bunch of parsley stalks
bay leaves
45 ml (3 tablespoons) oil
25 g (1 oz) margarine
2 medium onions, peeled and chopped
2 stalks celery, thinly sliced
2 cloves garlic, peeled and crushed
2 medium aubergines, finely diced
2 medium carrots, finely diced
675-g (1½-lb) can tomatoes
60 ml (4 tablespoons) tomato purée
10 ml (2 teaspoons) dried oregano
5 ml (1 teaspoon) dark Muscovado sugar
salt and pepper

For the cheese sauce
25 g (1 oz) butter
25 g (1 oz) flour
450 ml (¾ pint) milk
150 ml (¼ pint) plain yoghurt
3 eggs, beaten
a pinch of nutmeg
150 g (5 oz) cottage cheese

Put the lentils in a pan with the water, parsley stalks and bay leaves, bring to the boil and simmer for 50 minutes, or until they are tender but not mushy. Discard the herbs and drain off any water that has not been absorbed.

Heat the oil and margarine in a pan and fry the onions, celery and garlic over moderate heat for 3–4 minutes, stirring occasionally. Add the aubergines and carrots and stir-fry for 2–3 minutes. Cover the pan, lower the heat and cook gently for 10 minutes, stirring once or twice. Add the tomatoes, tomato purée, oregano and sugar, increase the heat and bring to the boil. Simmer uncovered for 10 minutes. Add the lentils, season well with salt and pepper and remove from the heat.

Cook the macaroni in boiling, salted water for 10 minutes, or until it is just tender. Drain.

To make the cheese sauce, melt the butter in a pan and stir in the flour. When it forms a roux, gradually pour on the milk, stirring all the time. Bring to the boil, still stirring, and simmer for 3 minutes. Remove from the heat and beat in the yoghurt, eggs, nutmeg and cottage cheese.

Now put it all together! Pour a layer of the lentil sauce into a large well-greased ovenproof dish, cover with macaroni and sprinkle on a little of the Parmesan cheese. Add more layers of lentil sauce, macaroni, and Parmesan cheese, finishing with the lentil sauce. Cover with the cheese sauce. If it's nearly full, stand the dish on a baking tray – saves spillages.

Bake in a pre-heated oven, 200°C (400°F), Gas 6, for 50 minutes, until the topping is a deep, deep brown. Serve hot. *Serves 8*

* This is amazingly good cold, too, served in thick slices with a salad.

MACARONI FLAN

It's a macaroni flan *case* actually, with a creamy vegetable filling.

> 175 g (6 oz) short-cut wholewheat macaroni
> salt
> 25 g (1 oz) butter
> 30 ml (2 tablespoons) chopped fresh parsley
> 25 g (1 oz) Parmesan cheese, grated
>
> *For the filling*
> 30 ml (2 tablespoons) oil
> 2 medium onions, peeled and thinly sliced
> 1 clove garlic, peeled and crushed
> 2 stalks celery, thinly sliced
> 2 medium courgettes, thinly sliced
> 50 g (2 oz) button mushrooms, sliced
> 175 g (6 oz) frozen peas, thawed
> 10 ml (2 teaspoons) dried oregano
> pepper
> 50 g (2 oz) cheese, grated
> 2 eggs
> 300 ml (½ pint) plain yoghurt
> 2 large tomatoes, thinly sliced

Cook the macaroni in boiling, salted water for 10 minutes, or until it is just tender. Drain and toss it with the butter, parsley and cheese. Press the mixture into a greased 20-cm (8-in) flan ring on a greased baking sheet.

To make the filling, heat the oil in a pan and fry the onion, garlic and celery over moderate heat for 3 minutes, stirring once or twice. Add the courgettes and fry to brown them lightly, then add the mushrooms and stir-fry for about 2 minutes. Stir in the peas and oregano and remove from the heat. Season well with pepper.

Sprinkle the grated cheese on the flan case and cover with the vegetable mixture. Beat together the eggs and yoghurt and season with salt and pepper. Pour this custard mixture over the vegetables. Arrange the tomato slices on top.

Bake in a pre-heated oven, 180°C (350°F), Gas 4, for 45 minutes, or until the filling is set. Serve warm, with a green salad.

Serves 4

* The 'flan case' can be prepared in advance and the vegetable filling cooked, ready to assemble and bake at the last minute.

COME-AGAIN SALAD

So named because that's what someone asked to do, when I served them my latest experimental salad!

> 100 g (4 oz) wholewheat pasta shells, or other pasta shapes
> salt
> 45 ml (3 tablespoons) Vinaigrette dressing (page 54)
> 3 dessert apples, cored and thinly sliced
> 30 ml (2 tablespoons) lemon juice
> 100 g (4 oz) dried stoned dates, chopped

75 ml (3 tablespoons) pecan halves
150 ml (¼ pint) soured cream
15 ml (1 tablespoon) chopped fresh mint

For serving
spinach leaves

For garnish
watercress

Cook the pasta in boiling, salted water for 12 minutes, or until it is just tender. Drain the shells with special care, to shake out the water trapped in the hollows. Toss the pasta while it's still hot, in the dressing. Leave to cool.

Toss the apples in the lemon juice, then stir in the dates and pecans. Add the pasta and mix thoroughly. Stir together the soured cream and mint and mix it into the salad. Pile the mixture decoratively on the spinach leaves and garnish with the watercress.

Serves 4

PASTA AND BEAN SALAD

It's a meal in itself, but an accompanying tomato salad with onion rings and lots of fresh basil does wonders, visually.

175 g (6 oz) short-cut wholewheat macaroni, or other
    pasta shapes
salt
1 avocado, stoned, skinned and sliced
105 ml (7 tablespoons) Vinaigrette dressing (page 54)
225 g (8 oz) young mange-tout peas, trimmed
450 g (1 lb) broad beans, shelled
pepper, freshly ground

For garnish
watercress

Cook the macaroni in boiling, salted water for 10 minutes, or until it is just tender. Just before the pasta is cooked, toss the avocado slices in the dressing, lift them out with a draining spoon and set them aside. Drain the macaroni and, while still hot, toss it in the dressing. Leave to cool.

Cook the peas and broad beans, separately, for about 7 minutes, or until they are barely tender. Drain them and allow to cool.

Toss the pasta, peas and beans together and grind on lots of pepper. Pile the salad on to a dish and arrange the avocado in a wheel pattern over it. Arrange the watercress sprigs in the centre.

Serves 4

5   Pastry

There's something so absolutely *right* about pastry made with wholewheat flour. Once you've tried it, and family and friends have found how delicious it is, you'll never look back.

Recipes in this chapter show that with 100 per cent wholewheat flour you can make shortcrust pastry that is a melt-in-the-mouth container for creamy vegetable mixtures and golden fruit concoctions. Make it into flans, quiches, pasties and double-crust pies; flavour it with cheese, nuts or spices for every-day-of-the-week variations. And for some top-crust pies and good old-fashioned roly-polys, substitute 81 per cent self-raising flour for a lighter, spongier texture.

There's no mystique about making wholewheat pastry, though there is quite a lot of myth. Follow the basic recipe (which is virtually identical to any shortcrust recipe), handle the pastry as little as possible, and chill it before rolling and shaping. Use the rolling-pin technique (page 107) to lift and lower the pastry into position – it's reassuringly simple.

The absorption rate of flours varies considerably, so sprinkle the water evenly over the dry ingredients, mix it in quickly and be prepared to *feel* the dough. You know you want a firm, pliable non-sticky paste, and you might have to use a little more or less water next time (or when you change your brand of flour) to achieve it. These pastry recipes have been tested using Allinson's stoneground plain 100 per cent wholewheat and stoneground self-raising 81 per cent farm-house flours.

If you have a food processor, the going's easy. It's probably best to make the pastry 'by hand' the first time, note exactly the amount of water needed, then next time twirl it all together in the processor.

Confidence gained – and appetites stimulated – with shortcrust can be transferred to rich flan pastry, with the addition of an egg yolk and, optionally, sugar. Slightly more difficult to roll, this rich pastry – but there's a handy technique to help (page 108).

On to puff pastry, an adaptation of the standard refined-flour recipe. This one has the butter fully rubbed into the flour but cannot – unfortunately – avoid the roll and turn and chill and wait part that prevents the fat from melting under the strain. It is, undoubtedly, a pastry for those who enjoy the therapy of cooking, or for wintry days when the kitchen's the place to be.

For fibre of a different kind, there's a pastry that combines medium oatmeal with wholewheat flour – it's delightfully crumbly and spans the range of sweet and savoury fillings. Try it, mix-and-match style, with fillings given for other pastries.

And lastly, there's choux pastry, in which 81 per cent extraction self-raising flour gives lovely puffed-up éclairs, buns or rings, all ready to turn into cocktail bouchées and teatime treats, or substantial main dishes. It's one of the simplest of all pastry techniques – more like making a sauce, really, and of course involves no rolling. So it's very well worth a triumphant try.

WHOLEWHEAT SHORTCRUST PASTRY

If you're a newcomer to making this most delicious of container-crusts, you might find it slightly crumbly, and a little difficult to handle, but well worth a second try, by which time you'll be shaping up to it like an expert!

175 g (6 oz) wholewheat flour
a large pinch of salt
75 g (3 oz) margarine, butter, white vegetable fat, or a
   mixture
about 45 ml (3 tablespoons) water

Mix together the flour and salt in a bowl and rub in the fat until the mixture is like fine, dry crumbs. Use just enough water to bind it to a firm dough – different flours absorb differing amounts, so this will vary. Shape the paste into a roll, close-wrap it in film or foil and chill it in the refrigerator for about 30 minutes. (When time is short, you needn't; but it does make the paste easier to roll and handle.) Then stand it in room temperature for about 10 minutes before rolling.

Roll the dough on a very lightly-floured board, as required for the recipe, handling it as little as possible. If it helps you, wrap the rolled-out paste around the rolling pin, then unroll to lower it over the flan case or pie dish. If the paste breaks, dampen the edges and press them together to seal. No harm done!

Ready-rubbed shortcrust mixture will keep in a covered container in the refrigerator for 7–8 days. Ready-shaped dough – a lined flan case – can be stored, close-wrapped in film or foil, for 2–3 days before baking. Both may be frozen.

* For cheese shortcrust, stir 50 g (2 oz) grated cheese into the rubbed-in ingredients.
* For extra-nutty shortcrust, stir 50 g (2 oz) ground nuts, such as blanched almonds or peanuts, into the rubbed-in flour and fat.
* For spiced shortcrust pastry, mix 5 ml (1 teaspoon) ground mixed spice, cinnamon or ginger into the dry ingredients.
* For a 'spongy shortcrust', a lighter pastry, ideally suited to baked or steam roly-polys, substitute 81 per cent self-raising flour.

RICH WHOLEWHEAT FLAN PASTRY

Use it as an alternative to shortcrust pastry. It's higher in protein and calories, level on fibre.

175 g (6 oz) wholewheat flour
a large pinch of salt
100 g (4 oz) margarine
1 egg yolk
about 15 ml (1 tablespoon) water

Mix together the flour and salt in a bowl and rub in the margarine until the mixture is like slightly sticky crumbs. Mix together the egg yolk and water and stir it in to make a firm dough. Lightly flour your hands and a working board and gently knead the paste until it is smooth. Close-wrap it in film or foil and chill for about 1 hour.

This pastry, with its higher fat content, is more difficult to roll. Place it between 2 sheets of greaseproof paper, polythene or foil and roll it with short, smooth strokes. To line a flan case or pie dish, remove the top sheet, lift the pastry up on the lower one and invert it on to the dish.

* For sweet rich pastry, stir in 25 g (1 oz) light Muscovado sugar before adding the egg yolk and water.
* For rich nut pastry, stir 50 g (2 oz) ground nuts, such as blanched almonds or hazelnuts, into the rubbed-in ingredients. Use nuts in the pastry with or without the sugar, as you prefer.
* For cheese pastry, stir 50 g (2 oz) grated cheese and a pinch of cayenne pepper or celery seed into the rubbed-in ingredients.

WHOLEWHEAT PUFF PASTRY

Here's the one to use for deep-dish pies with creamy vegetable fillings (page 125) or farmhouse fruit mixtures, or for sweet or savoury mille-feuilles.

225 g (8 oz) wholewheat flour
a pinch of salt
200 g (7 oz) butter, cut into small pieces
about 150 ml (¼ pint) water

Mix together the flour and salt in a bowl and rub in the butter. Mix to a stiff dough with the water. Roll out the dough on a very lightly-floured board to a thickness of 12 mm (½ in). Fold the pastry over, both ends to the middle. Give the dough a half-turn and roll out again. Fold it sides to middle again. Close-wrap it in film or foil and chill in the refrigerator for 30 minutes.

Roll out the dough; fold it; give it a half-turn; roll; fold; and chill for 30 minutes again.

Repeat this operation twice more. The dough is then ready to shape.

Roll and shape the pastry according to the recipe. Always leave it in a cool place for a further 30 minutes before baking, to avoid shrinkage.

OAT PASTRY

This pastry, with its half-and-half flour and oatmeal mixture, is perfect for both sweet and savoury dishes.

75 g (3 oz) medium oatmeal
75 g (3 oz) wholewheat flour
a pinch of salt
100 g (4 oz) hard margarine, chilled
1 egg, lightly beaten

Stir the oatmeal, flour and salt together in a bowl. Grate the margarine into the mixture and bind to a firm dough with the egg. Knead lightly to form a ball.

Turn the dough on to a lightly-floured board and roll it as required. The pastry has a very crumbly texture at this stage. To transfer it to the pie plate or dish, wrap it round the rolling pin then lower it into place.

CHOUX PASTRY

It won't be quite as fluffy as a cloud, but this pastry rises well and opens up a wealth of new possibilities.

    100 g (4 oz) 81 per cent self-raising flour
    a pinch of salt
    50 g (2 oz) butter
    150 ml (¼ pint) water
    3 eggs

Sift the flour and salt on to a piece of paper. Melt the butter and water in a small pan, bring to the boil then tip in the flour and stir vigorously until the mixture forms a ball. Allow to cool a little then beat in the eggs one at a time until the mixture is stiff and glossy (you may not need all of the third egg). Beat well.

Choux pastry can be piped into a ring, to be filled with a creamy vegetable sauce and served as a main dish, with other vegetables and a salad. Or it can be baked into puffy round buns, to fill with sweet or savoury mixtures: chocolate cream for éclairs; asparagus cream cheese for cocktail savouries, for example.

CARROT RING FLAN (*photograph on the front cover*)

1 recipe Wholewheat shortcrust pastry (page 106)

For the filling
750 g (1½ lb) carrots
salt
40 g (1½ oz) butter
25 g (1 oz) wholewheat flour
450 ml (¾ pint) single cream
50 g (2 oz) Gruyère cheese, grated
30 ml (2 tablespoons) chopped fresh mint
pepper

Cook the carrots in boiling, salted water, or steam them, until they are just tender.

Melt 25 g (1 oz) of the butter in a pan, stir in the flour and when it forms a roux, gradually pour on the cream, stirring all the time. Bring to the boil and simmer very gently for 3 minutes. Remove from the heat and stir in the cheese and mint. Season the sauce with pepper. Chop half the carrots finely and stir them into the sauce. Slice the remaining carrots thinly.

Roll out the pastry and line a 20-cm (8-in) flan dish. Prick the base all over with a fork and bake in a pre-heated oven, 180°C (350°F), Gas 4, for 30 minutes. Remove from the oven.

Increase the oven heat to 190°C (375°F), Gas 5. Spread the cheese and carrot sauce into the flan case and arrange the carrot slices on the top. Melt the remaining butter and brush this over the carrots. Return the flan to the oven and bake for 10 minutes. Serve warm.

Serves 4

AUBERGINE AND MACARONI FLAN

1 recipe Wholewheat shortcrust pastry (page 106)

For the filling
175 g (6 oz) short-cut wholewheat macaroni
salt
1 large aubergine, thinly sliced
15 ml (1 tablespoon) oil
50 g (2 oz) margarine
40 g (1½ oz) wholewheat flour
450 ml (¾ pint) milk
pepper
100 g (4 oz) Cheddar cheese, grated
2 hard-boiled eggs, chopped

Make the pastry as described. Roll it and line a 20-cm (8-in) flan dish. Prick the pastry base all over with a fork.

To make the filling, cook the macaroni in plenty of boiling, salted water for about 12–13 minutes, or until it is just tender. Plunge into cold water, drain and cool. Brush the aubergine slices lightly on both sides with oil, arrange them in a single layer on a baking sheet and bake in a pre-heated oven, 190°C (375°F), Gas 5, for 8 minutes, turning them once. Set aside to cool.

Melt the margarine in a pan. Stir in the flour and when it forms a roux, gradually pour on the milk. Bring to the boil, stirring, and simmer for 3 minutes. Season the sauce with salt and pepper, stir in half the cheese, the chopped eggs and the macaroni.

To assemble the flan, spread the macaroni mixture over the pastry case. Arrange overlapping slices of aubergine on the top, and sprinkle them with the remaining cheese. Cover the top with foil. Bake in the oven for 30 minutes, remove the foil and continue baking for 10 minutes, until the cheese is bubbling and golden. Serve warm.

Serves 4

MUSHROOM AND SOURED-CREAM QUICHE

Cream and brown and very farmhouse-looking, this flan goes well with a crisp green salad with perhaps basil-flavoured tomatoes.

1 recipe Wholewheat shortcrust pastry (page 106)

For the filling
25 g (1 oz) margarine
1 small onion, peeled and finely chopped
225 g (8 oz) button mushrooms, sliced
50 g (2 oz) cheese, grated
3 eggs
150 ml (¼ pint) plain yoghurt
150 ml (¼ pint) single cream
15 ml (1 tablespoon) chopped chives
salt and pepper

Roll out the pastry, line a 20-cm (8-in) flan case and prick the base all over with a fork. Bake, unfilled, in a pre-heated oven, 180°C (350°F), Gas 4, for 15 minutes.

Melt the margarine in a pan and fry the onion over moderate heat for 2–3 minutes. Add the mushrooms, reserving 8 of the largest slices for garnish, and cook for a further 2–3 minutes, stirring once or twice. Leave to cool.

Sprinkle the cheese over the partly-baked flan case then spread on the mushroom mixture. Beat together the eggs, yoghurt, cream and chives and season with salt and pepper. Pour the custard mixture into the flan case and arrange the reserved mushroom slices.

Return the flan to the oven and bake for 40–45 minutes, or until the custard is set. Serve warm.
Serves 4

SUMMER VEGETABLE QUICHE

You can vary the vegetable selection as the seasons change.
Try always to include some legumes – frozen or canned ones
or cooked dried pulses take well to this presentation.

1 recipe Wholewheat shortcrust pastry (page 106)

For the filling
3 medium carrots, thinly sliced
350 g (12 oz) broad beans, shelled (or use 175 g (6 oz)
    frozen broad beans, thawed)
3 medium courgettes, thinly sliced
salt
50 g (2 oz) cheese, grated
30 ml (2 tablespoons) chopped fresh parsley
100 g (4 oz) canned sweetcorn, drained
3 eggs
150 ml (¼ pint) milk
150 ml (¼ pint) single cream
pepper

For garnish
watercress sprigs

Roll out the pastry and use it to line a 20-cm (9-in) flan case.
Prick the base all over with a fork and bake the case in a pre-
heated oven, 180°C (350°F), Gas 4, for 15 minutes.

Cook the carrots, broad beans and courgettes in boiling,
salted water (or steam them) until they are only just tender.
Drain the vegetables, plunge them into cold water to
prevent further cooking, and drain again. Toss the courgettes on kitchen paper to dry them.

Sprinkle the cheese and parsley over the flan case. Make
neat rings of carrots, broad beans and courgettes, pressing
the vegetables well into the cheese. Spread the sweetcorn to

fill the centre. Beat together the eggs, milk and cream and season with salt and pepper. Slowly pour the custard mixture over the vegetables, taking care that they do not rise from the flan base.

Return the flan to the oven and bake for 40–45 minutes, or until the custard is set. Shorten the sprigs of watercress and arrange them in the centre of the flan. Serve warm. *Serves 4*

SPICED VEGETABLE PASTIES

Picnic or packed-lunch fare.

Wholewheat shortcrust pastry made with 225 g (8 oz) flour (page 106)

For the filling
225 g (8 oz) small potatoes, scrubbed
225 g (8 oz) carrots, diced
2 stalks celery, thinly sliced
60 ml (4 tablespoons) frozen peas, thawed
salt
25 g (1 oz) margarine
2.5 ml (½ teaspoon) ground ginger
10 ml (2 teaspoons) ground coriander
a pinch of ground cloves
pepper
50 g (2 oz) button mushrooms, sliced
90 ml (6 tablespoons) soured cream
milk, for brushing

To make the filling, cook the potatoes, carrots, celery and peas in boiling, salted water (or steam them) until they are all just tender. (You can of course use small amounts of ready-cooked vegetables.) Drain. Dice the potatoes.

Melt the margarine in a pan and stir in the spices and mushrooms. Cook over moderate heat for 2 minutes, then add the other vegetables and stir well to coat them. Set aside to cool, then stir in the soured cream and season with salt.

Roll out the pastry and cut 4 circles about 17.5 cm (7 in) in diameter. Dampen the rims. Divide the filling between the pastry rounds, piling it on to one side only. Fold the pastry circles over to enclose the filling and press the edges together to seal. Brush the tops with milk. Re-roll the pastry trimmings, cut leaf shapes, arrange them on the pasties and brush them with milk.

Place the pasties on a greased baking sheet. Bake in a pre-heated oven, 200°C (400°F), Gas 6, for 25 minutes. Serve warm or cold.

Makes 4 pasties

DOUBLE-CRUST WATERCRESS PIE

Wholewheat shortcrust pastry made with 225 g (8 oz) flour (page 106)

For the filling
225 g (8 oz) potatoes, scrubbed
2 medium carrots, scrubbed
175 g (6 oz) cheese, grated
salt and pepper
3 eggs, beaten
2 bunches watercress, trimmed and chopped
2 spring onions, peeled and thinly sliced

Steam or boil the potatoes and carrots until they are just tender, then dice them finely. Leave them to cool, then mix with the cheese and season with salt and pepper. Beat in the eggs, reserving a little to glaze.

Roll out the pastry and use two-thirds of it to line a greased 18-cm (7-in) pie plate. Pour in the vegetable filling and cover with the watercress and onion. Dampen the pastry edge and cover with the remaining piece. Pinch the edges to seal and brush the top with beaten egg. Cut leaf shapes from the pastry trimmings, arrange them on the top of the pie and brush with egg. Make a hole in the centre of the pie.

Bake in a pre-heated oven, 200°C (400°F), Gas 6, for 30 minutes. Serve cold, with perhaps tomato and basil salad or red cabbage and sultana salad.

Serves 4

SPICED APPLE AND NUT FLAN

  1 recipe Spiced shortcrust pastry (page 107), with ground
     cinnamon

  For the filling
  450 g (1 lb) dessert apples, cored and thinly sliced
  50 g (2 oz) Demerara sugar
  2.5 ml (½ teaspoon) ground cinnamon
  50 g (2 oz) raisins
  50 g (2 oz) cashew nuts
  milk, for brushing

Roll out the pastry on a lightly-floured board and line a greased 20-cm (8-in) flan ring placed on a greased baking sheet. Arrange the apple slices in rings on the pastry. Mix together the sugar, cinnamon, raisins and nuts and sprinkle this mixture on the apples. Re-roll the trimmings and cut them into thin strips. Dampen the pastry rim and press on the strips. Brush all over the pastry with milk.

Bake in a pre-heated oven, 180°C (350°F), Gas 4, for 45 minutes, or until the pastry is well browned. Serve hot or cold.

Serves 6

PECAN PIE

An old favourite that comes out with high marks in the fibre context.

Wholewheat shortcrust pastry made with 225 g (8 oz) flour (page 106)

For the filling
4 eggs, lightly beaten
225 g (8 oz) molasses
50 g (2 oz) margarine
15 ml (1 tablespoon) lemon juice
100 g (4 oz) chopped pecans
50 g (2 oz) pecan halves

Roll out the pastry and line a deep 23-cm (9-in) pie plate.

Reserve a little beaten egg for brushing. Melt the molasses and the margarine in a pan with the lemon juice and stir until well blended. Allow to cool, then beat in the eggs and chopped nuts. Pour the mixture into the pastry case. Brush the pastry edge with the reserved beaten egg.

Bake the pie in a pre-heated oven, 190°C (375°F), Gas 5, for 30 minutes. Remove the pie from the oven; reduce the heat to 160°C (325°F), Gas 3. Arrange the pecan halves on the top of the pie and bake for a further 20 minutes. Serve cold.

Serves 6–8

MINCEMEAT FLAN

First make your mincemeat (page 231). It's a tasty store-cupboard stand-by for a flan that's packed with fibre.

1 recipe Wholewheat nut shortcrust pastry (page 106), with ground almonds

For the filling
225 g (8 oz) mincemeat (page 231)
50 g (2 oz) wholewheat breadcrumbs
25 g (1 oz) Demerara sugar
grated rind of 1 orange
25 g (1 oz) butter, melted

Roll out the pastry and line a 20-cm (8-in) greased flan dish. Spread the mincemeat over the pastry. Mix together the breadcrumbs, sugar, orange rind and butter and scatter over the mincemeat.

Bake the flan in a pre-heated oven, 200°C (400°F), Gas 6, for 25 minutes. Serve hot or cold.
Serves 6

EGG AND SWEETCORN PIE

Baked jacket potatoes go well with this.

1 recipe Spongy shortcrust pastry (page 107)

For the filling
25 g (1 oz) margarine
25 g (1 oz) wholewheat flour
300 ml (½ pint) milk, or single cream
60 ml (4 tablespoons) double cream
salt and pepper
4 hard-boiled eggs

225-g (8-oz) can sweetcorn, drained
3 tomatoes, skinned and sliced
175 g (6 oz) cheese, grated
30 ml (2 tablespoons) chopped fresh parsley

Roll out the pastry to fit the top of a 1-litre (1¾-pint) deep pie dish. Make a sauce with the margarine, flour and milk. Bring to the boil, simmer for 3 minutes, then stir in the cream and season with salt and pepper. Remove from the heat.

Mix together in a bowl the eggs, sweetcorn, tomatoes, cheese and parsley; pour on the sauce and mix well. Put a pie funnel into the prepared pie dish and spoon the cheese mixture round it. Grease the rim of the dish, cut a 2.5-cm (1-in) wide strip of pastry and press it on to the rim. Dampen the pastry strip, put the pastry lid in place, fitting it over the funnel, and brush it with a little milk. Cut leaf shapes from the pastry trimmings, arrange them on the pie and brush them with milk.

Bake the pie in a pre-heated oven, 200°C (400°F), Gas 6, for 35–40 minutes, or until the pastry is crisp and golden brown. Serve hot.
Serves 6

VEGETABLE ROLY-POLY

Spongy shortcrust pastry made with 225 g (8 oz) self-raising flour (page 107)

For the filling
25 g (1 oz) margarine
1 small onion, peeled and finely chopped
2 small leeks, well washed and very thinly sliced
2 tomatoes, skinned and chopped

100 g (4 oz) mushrooms, chopped
10 ml (2 teaspoons) wholewheat flour
15 ml (1 tablespoon) chopped fresh parsley
25 g (1 oz) chopped walnuts
60 ml (4 tablespoons) double cream
salt and pepper
15 ml (1 tablespoon) yeast extract
milk, for brushing

Roll out the pastry to a rectangle 30 × 18 cm (12 × 7 in).

Melt the margarine in a pan and fry the onion and leeks over moderate heat for 3–4 minutes, stirring now and then. Add the tomatoes and mushrooms and cook for a further 3 minutes, stirring occasionally. Stir in the flour, cook for 2 minutes, then add the parsley, walnuts and cream and season with salt and pepper. Allow to cool.

Spread the yeast extract over the pastry. Spread on the filling, leaving a margin of 2.5 cm (1 in) all round. Dampen the pastry edges. Roll up from one short side, to make a 'Swiss-roll'. Press the edges together to seal and brush the pastry with milk.

Place the roll on a greased baking sheet and bake in a pre-heated oven, 200°C (400°F), Gas 6, for 30–35 minutes, or until the pastry is well risen and crisp. Serve hot.
Serves 4–6

* As an alternative, you can wrap the roll in foil (omit brushing the pastry with milk) and steam it for $1\frac{1}{2}$–$1\frac{3}{4}$ hours.
* Tomato sauce (page 261) or Béchamel sauce go well.

FLAPJACK FLAN

1 recipe Rich nut flan pastry (page 108), with ground hazelnuts

For the filling
120 ml (8 tablespoons) clear honey
40 g (1½ oz) butter
grated rind and juice of 1 lemon
90 ml (6 tablespoons) Muesli base (1) or (2) (page 61)
2 dessert apples, cored and finely chopped
milk, for brushing

Roll out the pastry on a lightly-floured board and line a greased 20-cm (8-in) pie plate.

Melt the honey and butter in a pan with the lemon rind and lemon juice and stir in the muesli and apples. Spread this mixture over the pastry. Flute the edges and brush them with milk.

Bake in a pre-heated oven, 180°C (350°F), Gas 4, for 25–30 minutes. Serve warm or cold.
Serves 4–6

HARVEST CREAM FLAN

1 recipe Rich nut flan pastry (page 108), with ground almonds

For the filling
225 g (8 oz) mixed dried fruit (e.g. apple rings, apricots, pears, prunes), soaked overnight and drained
150 g (6 oz) cream cheese
50 g (2 oz) light Muscovado sugar
3 eggs
150 ml (¼ pint) double cream
5 ml (1 teaspoon) grated lemon rind
30 ml (2 tablespoons) Demerara sugar

Roll out the pastry and line a 20-cm (8-in) flan case.

To make the filling, beat together the cheese and sugar.

Beat in the eggs one at a time, then the cream and lemon rind. Spread the mixture over the flan case. Pat the fruit dry, arrange it over the cream filling and sprinkle with the Demerara sugar.

Bake the flan in a pre-heated oven, 180°C (350°F), Gas 4, for 35–40 minutes, or until the filling is set. (Test by inserting a knife. It should come out clean.) Serve cold. *Serves 6*

ALMOND FLAN

Rich nut pastry and a light, spongy-textured fruit filling make a compelling combination.

 1 recipe Rich nut flan pastry (page 108), with ground almonds and sugar

For the filling
50 g (2 oz) seedless raisins
50 g (2 oz) sultanas
25 g (1 oz) mixed, chopped candied peel
50 g (2 oz) blanched flaked almonds
50 g (2 oz) margarine
50 g (2 oz) light Muscovado sugar
1 egg
1 egg white
50 g (2 oz) ground almonds
a few drops of almond essence (optional)

Roll out the pastry and line a 20-cm (8-in) greased flan ring, placed on a greased baking sheet. Prick the base all over with a fork.

To make the filling, mix together the raisins, sultanas, chopped peel and flaked almonds. Beat together the margarine, sugar, egg, egg white, ground almonds and almond essence if using. When the mixture is smooth and shiny stir in the dried fruits. Pour the filling into the pastry case and level the top.

Bake in a pre-heated oven, 180°C (350°F), Gas 4, for 35–40 minutes, or until the filling is well risen and set. Leave on a baking tray to cool.
Serves 6

COCONUT SLICE

   1 recipe Rich flan pastry (page 108)

For the filling
100 g (4 oz) grated coconut, or coconut shreds
75 g (3 oz) seedless raisins
1 egg, beaten
25 g (1 oz) light Muscovado sugar
milk, for brushing

Roll out the pastry to a 30-cm (12-in) square and cut off a 2.5-cm (1-in) strip from one side.

Beat together the filling ingredients and spread the mixture down the centre of the pastry. Dampen the edges and fold the two sides to meet in the middle, over the filling. Press the join together and dampen it. Twist the pastry strip into a rope and press it along the join. Brush the pastry with milk.

Place on a greased baking sheet and bake in a pre-heated oven, 200°C (400°F), Gas 6, for 25 minutes, or until the pastry is crisp and golden brown. Serve cold.
Serves 6–8

OLD-FASHIONED VEGETABLE PIE

A rich, flaky pie crust hides a selection of fresh, seasonal vegetables in a lightly-spiced sauce. It's the perfect dish to serve on a big occasion.

1 recipe Wholewheat puff pastry (page 109)

For the filling
225 g (8 oz) potatoes, scrubbed
225 g (8 oz) carrots, scrubbed
225 g (8 oz) parsnips, scrubbed
1 medium cauliflower, cut into florets
225 g (8 oz) frozen broad beans, thawed
salt
225 g (8 oz) canned sweetcorn, drained
30 ml (2 tablespoons) chopped fresh parsley

For the sauce
40 g (1½ oz) margarine
20 ml (4 teaspoons) wholewheat flour
10 ml (2 teaspoons) mild curry powder
5 ml (1 teaspoon) ground coriander
300 ml (½ pint) single cream
salt and pepper

Steam or boil the fresh and frozen vegetables in salted water until they are just tender. Plunge them into cold water to prevent further cooking, drain, and mix them with the sweetcorn and parsley. Dice and set aside.

To make the sauce, melt the margarine and stir in the flour and spices. When a roux is formed, gradually pour on the cream, stirring until the sauce thickens. Season with salt and pepper and leave to cool.

Stir the sauce into the vegetables. Put a pie funnel into a deep 2-litre (3½-pint) pie dish and spoon the vegetables round it. Grease the rim of the dish.

Roll out the pastry on a lightly-floured board. Cut off a 2.5-cm (1-in) strip and press this on to the rim. Dampen the pastry strip and lower on the pastry topping. Press the edges together and flute all round. Brush the pastry with beaten egg. Re-roll the pastry trimmings, cut decorative leaf shapes, arrange them in place and brush them with egg to glaze. Leave for 30 minutes before baking.

Stand the dish on a baking sheet and bake in a pre-heated oven, 200°C (400°F), Gas 6, for 20–25 minutes, or until the pastry is golden brown. Serve hot.

Serves 6

CREAMY CHEESE MILLE-FEUILLE

An impressive savoury dish to serve as part of a cold buffet with lots of crunchy salads.

1 recipe Wholewheat puff pastry (page 109)

For the fillings
225 g (8 oz) cream cheese
10 ml (2 teaspoons) curry paste
2 bananas, mashed
225 g (8 oz) cottage cheese
50 g (2 oz) chopped walnuts
50 g (2 oz) stoned dried dates, chopped
45 ml (3 tablespoons) soured cream, beaten
2 oranges, peeled and segmented

For garnish
watercress sprigs

Roll out the pastry on a lightly-floured board and cut into three pieces about 23 x 11.5 cm (9 x 4½ in); place them on baking sheets, prick all over with a fork and leave to rest for 30 minutes in the refrigerator.

Bake the pastry in a pre-heated oven, 220°C (425°F), Gas 7, for 12 minutes. Cool the pastry on a wire rack. You can then store it in an airtight tin for 2–3 days if you wish.

To make the fillings, beat together in a bowl the cream cheese, curry paste and bananas. In another bowl, beat together the cottage cheese, walnuts and dates.

Now it's assembly time! Spread one of the fillings on one layer of pastry. Cover that with another piece of pastry and spread that one with the second filling. Cover with the last pastry layer. Spread the soured cream over the top and arrange the orange segments in a row. Garnish with the watercress sprigs.

Serves 8

* For a completely different effect, blend the cheeses with chopped fresh herbs, skinned tomatoes, canned pimentos, tomato purée and watercress sprigs.

VEGETABLE OATIES

Crumbly cheese and vegetable pasties that melt in the mouth.

1 recipe Oat pastry (page 109)

For the filling
225 g (8 oz) potatoes, scrubbed
225 g (8 oz) parsnips, scrubbed
30 ml (2 tablespoons) chopped fresh parsley
75 g (3 oz) cheese, grated
salt and pepper

For glazing
1 egg, beaten

Steam or boil the potatoes and parsnips until they are just

tender. Drain and dice finely. Leave to cool, then mix the vegetables with the parsley and cheese and season with salt and pepper.

Roll out the pastry thinly and cut into 6 × 10-cm (4-in) circles, and dampen the edges. Pile the vegetable filling into the centre of the pastry rounds, fold over two sides to meet in the middle and pinch the edges together in the traditional pasty manner. Brush with the beaten egg.

Arrange the pasties on a greased baking sheet and bake in a pre-heated oven, 200°C (400°F), Gas 6, for 20–25 minutes, or until golden brown. Serve hot or cold.
Makes 6 pasties

RAISIN AND WALNUT TART

There's a breath of the Highlands in this open tart which has a rich, moist filling to contrast with the crunchy oat pastry.

1 recipe Oat pastry (page 109)

For the filling
75 g (3 oz) butter
75 g (3 oz) dark Muscovado sugar
15 ml (1 tablespoon) lemon juice
2 eggs
175 g (6 oz) raisins
50 g (2 oz) chopped walnuts

Roll out the pastry and line a greased 23-cm (9-in) tart tin. Flute the edges.

Beat together in a bowl the butter, sugar and lemon juice until the mixture is light and fluffy. Beat in the eggs one at a time, then the raisins and walnuts. Spread the mixture over the pastry and level the top.

Re-roll the pastry trimmings and cut large leaf shapes to decorate. Place them on the filling.

Bake the tart in a pre-heated oven, 190°C (375°F), Gas 5, for 25 minutes, or until the pastry is crisp and well browned. Serve warm or cold.

Serves 6

MUSHROOM ÉCLAIRS

1 recipe Choux pastry (page 110)

For the filling
50 g (2 oz) butter
1 small onion, peeled and finely chopped
1 clove garlic, peeled and crushed
30 ml (2 tablespoons) wholewheat flour
225 ml (8 fl oz) milk
225 g (8 oz) mushrooms, chopped
30 ml (2 tablespoons) chopped fresh parsley
salt and pepper
2 hard-boiled eggs, chopped

For garnish
watercress

Spoon the choux paste into a piping bag fitted with a plain 12-mm (½-in) nozzle. Pipe 7.5-cm (3-in) strips of the paste, well apart, on to a greased and floured baking sheet. Bake in a pre-heated oven, 200°C (400°F), Gas 6, for 15 minutes, or until the buns are well risen and dry.

While the buns are cooking, make the filling. Melt the butter in a pan, fry the onion and garlic over moderate heat for 3–4 minutes, stirring once or twice. Stir in the flour and, when it forms a roux, gradually pour on the milk, stirring all the time. Add the mushrooms and parsley, season with salt and pepper and simmer for 5 minutes, until the sauce thickens. Stir in the chopped eggs.

As soon as the buns are cooked, split them lengthways. Fill them with the sauce, arrange on a dish garnished with the watercress and serve hot.

Makes 8 éclairs

* Other vegetables can replace the mushrooms in the sauce. Thinly-sliced leeks, small-diced carrots, chopped watercress are all good.
* A crisp green or winter-roots salad goes well with these savoury éclairs. So do creamy mashed potatoes spiked with toasted almond flakes.

SPINACH CHOUX RING

   1 recipe Choux pastry (page 110)

   For the filling
   25 g (1 oz) butter
   225 g (8 oz) frozen spinach, thawed
   40 g (1½ oz) wholewheat flour
   300 ml (½ pint) milk
   150 ml (¼ pint) single cream
   100 g (4 oz) Wensleydale cheese, grated
   100 g (4 oz) cottage cheese
   a pinch of grated nutmeg
   salt and pepper
   2 hard-boiled eggs, chopped

Using two dessertspoons, pile the choux paste into a thick 20-cm (8-in) circle on a greased and floured baking sheet. Bake in a pre-heated oven, 200°C (400°F), Gas 6, for 35–40 minutes, or until the pastry ring is well puffed-up and deep golden brown in colour.

Make the filling while the pastry's cooking. Melt the butter in a pan and stir in the spinach, chopping it with a wooden spoon to break it up. Stir in the flour and then gradually pour on the milk and cream. Bring to the boil, lower the heat and simmer for 5 minutes. Stir in all the cheese and season the sauce with nutmeg, salt and pepper. When the cheese has melted, stir in the chopped eggs.

Split the choux ring in half horizontally as soon as it is baked. Fill the lower half with the spinach mixture, replace the top and serve at once.

Serves 4

* Baked tomatoes sprinkled with herbs and jacket-boiled potatoes go well with this recipe.

6 Filled Vegetables

One of the most appetizing ways to present a blend of grains, pulses, fruit, vegetables, herbs, nuts and seeds is in vegetable containers. Deep, deep purple and shiny-bright aubergines; toasty-brown roast onions; comfortably familiar jacket potatoes; elegantly constructed globe artichokes; neat little parcels wrapped Greek-style in vine leaves – there's a wonderful variety at our fingertips.

Many of these recipes use such relatively small amounts of cooked grains, pulses and vegetables that it's a chore to cook them specially. Plan ahead, cook more than you need for another dish and turn the left-overs into an imaginative filling. If a recipe suggests cooked rice and you have millet or wholewheat grains, no matter. If diced carrots are listed and you have parsnips, you could find they're even better. Good cooking is about making the most of the ingredients you have. Filled vegetables must be one of the most attractive and delicious ways to do that.

GLOBE ARTICHOKES WITH MUSHROOMS

These thistle-like heads with a nutty flavour make surely the most decorative containers of all.

    4 large globe artichokes
    45 ml (3 tablespoons) lemon juice
    salt

45 ml (3 tablespoons) oil
1 small onion, peeled and finely chopped
100 g (4 oz) button mushrooms, finely chopped
50 g (2 oz) pine nuts
50 g (2 oz) wholewheat breadcrumbs
15 ml (1 tablespoon) chopped fresh parsley
pepper
450 ml (¾ pint) vegetable stock (page 12)

Pull off and discard any tough or discoloured outer leaves. Gently open out the artichokes until you reveal the inner ring of soft leaves. Pull these out, then scrape out the bristly choke, using a teaspoon. Trim off the stalk to level the base and brush the inside and underside with lemon juice. Put the artichokes into a pan of boiling water with the remaining lemon juice, salt and 15 ml (1 tablespoon) of the oil. Cover and boil for 10 minutes, then drain thoroughly by standing them upside-down.

Melt the remaining oil in a pan and fry the onion for 2 minutes over moderate heat. Add the mushrooms, nuts and breadcrumbs, stir well and cook for 2 minutes. Stir in the parsley and season with salt and pepper.

Spoon the stuffing into the centre of the artichokes and close the outer leaves around it. Place the vegetables in a deep ovenproof dish and pour on the hot stock.

Bake, uncovered, in a pre-heated oven, 190°C (375°F), Gas 5, for 1 hour, basting often with the stock. Serve hot, with the stock as a sauce.
Serves 4

* As guests pull away each leaf, and scrape off the flesh at the base with their teeth, fingerbowls and napkins will be welcome.
* As an alternative prepare the artichokes as described and boil them with lemon juice, salt and oil for 45 minutes. Drain them, cool and fill the centres with a salad such as a

well-flavoured rice salad or watercress and diced avocado in mayonnaise.

AUBERGINE 'RATATOUILLE'

Mixed vegetable filling piled into the p   shells and grilled to a sizzle.

4 medium aubergines
salt
25 g (1 oz) margarine
1 small onion, peeled and finely chopped
1 clove garlic, peeled and crushed
1 medium courgette, finely chopped
1 red pepper, seeded and chopped
50 g (2 oz) mushrooms, chopped
75 g (3 oz) canned sweetcorn, drained
50 g (2 oz) cheese, grated
15 ml (1 tablespoon) chopped fresh parsley
pepper
3 large tomatoes, thinly sliced
15 ml (1 tablespoon) oil

Slice the aubergines in half lengthways. Scoop out the flesh, taking care not to pierce the skin. Put the flesh in a colander and sprinkle it with salt. Leave to drain for 30 minutes, then rinse under the cold tap, drain and pat dry.

Melt the margarine in a pan and fry the onion and garlic over moderate heat for 3–4 minutes, stirring once or twice. Stir in the courgette, pepper, mushrooms and aubergine and fry for 10 minutes, stirring often, then add the sweetcorn. Remove from the heat after 2–3 minutes, mix in the cheese and parsley and season generously with salt and pepper. Place the aubergine halves on the grill rack and pile in the filling. Arrange the sliced tomatoes on top and sprinkle with the oil.

Cook under the grill, pre-heated to high, for 6–7 minutes, until the filling is bubbling. Serve hot.
Serves 4

IMAM BAYALDI

Packed with fruit, vegetables, herbs and nuts, the aubergines are served cold.

2 large aubergines
salt
90 ml (6 tablespoons) olive oil
1 large onion, peeled and chopped
2 cloves garlic, peeled and crushed
5 ml (1 tablespoon) ground cumin
225 g (8 oz) tomatoes, skinned and chopped
45 ml (3 tablespoons) rolled oats
50 g (2 oz) blanched almonds
50 g (2 oz) seedless raisins
50 g (2 oz) sultanas
2.5 ml (½ teaspoon) ground cinnamon
pepper
30 ml (2 tablespoons) lemon juice
300 ml (½ pint) water

For garnish
1 lemon, quartered

Cut the aubergines in half lengthways and scoop out the flesh with a teaspoon, taking care not to pierce the walls. Put the aubergine flesh in a colander and sprinkle with salt. Leave to drain for 30 minutes. Rinse under cold, running water, drain and dry.

Heat 15 ml (1 tablespoon) of the oil and fry the onion and garlic over moderate heat for 2–3 minutes. Stir in the cumin and cook for 1 minute, then add the tomatoes, oats and aubergine flesh. Stir well and simmer for 10 minutes. Remove from the heat and stir in the almonds, raisins, sultanas and cinnamon. Season with salt and pepper. Pile the mixture into the aubergine shells.

Place the aubergines in a baking dish, pour round them the remaining oil, the lemon juice and water and cover the dish. Cook in a pre-heated oven, 180°C (350°F), Gas 4, for 1 hour. Cool and serve cold, with salad.

Serves 4

CABBAGE BOWL

Its best friends couldn't say that cabbage always presents well. This way it does! Jacket-boiled potatoes make a particularly good accompaniment.

    1 small, firm white or green cabbage
    salt
    50 g (2 oz) margarine
    2 medium onions, peeled and chopped
    1 clove garlic, peeled and crushed
    225 g (8 oz) carrots, grated
    100 g (4 oz) mushrooms, chopped
    100 g (4 oz) wholewheat breadcrumbs
    100 g (4 oz) chopped walnuts
    60 ml (4 tablespoons) vegetable stock (page 12)
    pepper
    30 ml (2 tablespoons) chopped fresh parsley
    1 hard-boiled egg, chopped

Trim the cabbage to a neat, round shape, discarding discoloured outer leaves (or using them for soup). Blanch the cabbage in boiling, salted water for 5 minutes, then drain it well and pat dry. Cool a little, then pull the cabbage apart at the centre. Without cutting through to the base, cut out the centre, to leave a large hollow – a curved grapefruit knife is useful. Chop the reclaimed cabbage finely.

Melt half the margarine in a pan and fry the onions and garlic over moderate heat for 3–4 minutes, stirring once or twice. Add the carrot, mushrooms, half the breadcrumbs, half the walnuts and the chopped cabbage, stir well and cook for 3 minutes. Stir in the stock, season with salt and pepper, cover and simmer for 10 minutes. Taste the filling and adjust the seasoning if needed. Stir in the parsley.

Spoon the filling into the hollow cabbage and wrap it closely in foil. Stand the cabbage on a trivet in a large pan half-filled with boiling water. Return the water quickly to the boil, cover and boil for 1 hour, topping up with more boiling water as required.

Melt the remaining margarine in a pan and fry the reserved breadcrumbs and walnuts, stirring often, until the mixture is dry. Stir in the chopped egg.

Unwrap the cabbage and press the topping over it. Serve it cut like a cake, in large wedges.

Serves 4

CHESTNUT AND CABBAGE ROLLS

Use other leaves, too – spinach or vine leaves make tasty little parcels.

12 leaves from a large cabbage
salt

For the filling
50 g (2 oz) margarine
1 medium onion, peeled and finely chopped
2 stalks celery, finely chopped
350 g (12 oz) chestnuts, skinned (or use dried ones, soaked and drained)

50 g (2 oz) wholewheat breadcrumbs
45 ml (3 tablespoons) chopped fresh parsley
5 ml (1 teaspoon) dried oregano
salt and pepper
a pinch of grated nutmeg
1 egg, lightly beaten

15 ml (1 tablespoon) tomato purée
300 ml (½ pint) vegetable stock, boiling (page 12)

Choose large, tender, undamaged inner leaves. Cut away the thick part of the stalk. Blanch them in boiling, salted water for 4 minutes, then plunge into cold water. Drain and pat dry.

To make the filling, melt the margarine in a pan and fry the onion and celery over moderate heat for 3–4 minutes, stirring once or twice. Liquidize, grind or mash the chestnuts and mix them with the breadcrumbs and herbs. Stir in the onion and celery and season with salt, pepper and nutmeg. Bind the mixture with the beaten egg.

Place the cabbage leaves on a board, put 1 large heaped tablespoon of the filling in the centre of each. Fold the stalk end over almost to enclose the filling. Fold each side to the middle, then roll up from the stalk end to make tight, neat parcels.

Place the parcels in a single layer in a large frying-pan and pour on the tomato purée mixed with the stock. Bring again to the boil, lower the heat, cover the pan and simmer for 50 minutes. Serve hot.
Serves 6

MARROW WITH LENTILS

175 g (6 oz) brown lentils, soaked and drained
45 ml (3 tablespoons) oil
1 large onion, peeled and chopped

1 clove garlic, peeled and crushed
2 stalks celery, thinly sliced
1 medium carrot, finely diced
1 red pepper, seeded and chopped
90 ml (6 tablespoons) cooked brown rice
5 ml (1 teaspoon) ground coriander
1 medium marrow
30 ml (2 tablespoons) chopped fresh parsley
150 ml (¼ pint) plain yoghurt
1 egg
50 g (2 oz) cheese, grated
salt and pepper

For serving
300 ml (½ pint) Tomato sauce (page 261)

Cook the lentils in unsalted water for 45–50 minutes, until they are just tender. Drain them well.

Heat the oil in a pan and fry the onion, garlic and celery over moderate heat for 3–4 minutes, stirring once or twice. Stir in the carrot and pepper and cook for a further 2 minutes. Remove the pan from the heat, stir in the lentils, rice and coriander and set aside to cool a little.

To prepare the marrow, cut off each end. Using a vegetable baller or a dessertspoon and working from each end to the middle, scoop out the seeds and some of the flesh, leaving 2.5-cm (1-in)-thick walls.

Beat the parsley, yoghurt, egg and cheese into the cooled filling mixture and season well with salt and pepper. Pack the filling into the marrow. Closely wrap it in foil and place in a baking dish.

Cook in a pre-heated oven, 180°C (350°F), Gas 4, for 1¼-1½ hours, or until the marrow is tender. Serve hot, with the tomato sauce.

Serves 6

ROAST ONIONS

Use the largest, juiciest onions you can find for a herby-lentil filling. Make good use of the oven to roast potatoes at the same time.

4 large Spanish onions, peeled
salt
25 g (1 oz) margarine
1 medium onion, peeled and finely chopped
1 clove garlic, peeled and crushed
225 g (8 oz) cooked brown lentils
10 ml (2 teaspoons) tomato purée
45 ml (3 tablespoons) vegetable stock (page 12)
5 ml (1 teaspoon) yeast extract
2 tomatoes, skinned and chopped
60 ml (4 tablespoons) wholewheat breadcrumbs
15 ml (1 tablespoon) chopped fresh mint
5 ml (1 teaspoon) dried oregano
pepper
40 g (1½ oz) cheese, grated

For serving
300 ml (½ pint) Tomato sauce (page 261)

Boil the Spanish onions in salted water for 10 minutes. Drain them, pat them thoroughly dry and leave to cool.

Melt the margarine in a pan and fry the chopped onion and garlic over moderate heat for 3–4 minutes, stirring once or twice. Stir in the lentils, tomato purée, stock and yeast extract and bring to the boil. Add the tomatoes and simmer gently for 5 minutes. Stir in 15 ml (1 tablespoon) of the breadcrumbs, the herbs, and season with salt and pepper.

Open out the onion centres and scoop out some of the flesh, leaving thick firm walls. Chop the onion flesh, stir it into the filling mixture, taste and adjust the seasoning if necessary. Spoon the filling into the onion cavities, piling it up into high domes. Mix together the remaining crumbs and the cheese and press this mixture on the top.

Place the onions in a greased baking dish and roast them in a pre-heated oven, 190°C (375°F), Gas 5, for 35 minutes, or until the topping is firm and crisp. Serve hot with the tomato sauce.

Serves 4

OLIVE PEPPERS

Glistening with shiny black olives and aromatic with herbs, a good dinner-party choice.

    4 large green or red peppers
    90 ml (6 tablespoons) oil
    2 spring onions, peeled and thinly sliced
    100 g (4 oz) cooked brown rice
    30 ml (2 tablespoons) seedless raisins
    12 black olives, stoned and chopped
    30 ml (2 tablespoons) chopped fresh parsley
    5 ml (1 teaspoon) dried basil, or oregano
    salt and pepper
    300 ml (½ pint) Tomato sauce (page 261)

For the topping
    60 ml (4 tablespoons) wholewheat breadcrumbs
    25 g (1 oz) grated Parmesan cheese
    a large pinch of paprika

Cut the tops from the peppers, scoop out the seeds, cut away the inner pith, wash and dry them.

Mix together 60 ml (4 tablespoons) of the oil with the onions, rice, raisins, olives and herbs and season with salt and pepper. Divide the mixture between the peppers and place them in a greased baking dish. Spoon 15 ml (1 tablespoon) of the tomato sauce on to each of the peppers, then sprinkle them with the remaining oil. Mix together the breadcrumbs, cheese and paprika and press the topping on to the peppers.

Bake in a pre-heated oven, 180°C (350°F), Gas 4, for 45 minutes. Serve hot, with the remaining tomato sauce.
Serves 4

* For a quicker version, blanch the prepared peppers in boiling, salted water for 4 minutes, then drain them. Fill them with left-over risotto, cover with a crumb topping or simply grated cheese and bake for 25 minutes.

HAZELNUT AND YOGHURT PEPPERS

4 large green or red peppers
50 g (2 oz) margarine
1 large onion, peeled and finely chopped
50 g (2 oz) wholewheat breadcrumbs
50 g (2 oz) prunes, stoned and chopped
225 g (8 oz) ground hazelnuts
15 ml (1 tablespoon) chopped fresh parsley
15 ml (1 tablespoon) chopped chives
a pinch of grated nutmeg
salt and pepper
1 egg, beaten

For the topping
150 ml (¼ pint) plain yoghurt
1 egg
salt and pepper

Cut a thin slice from the top of each pepper, scoop out the seeds and cut away the pith.

Melt the margarine in a pan and fry the onion over moderate heat for 3–4 minutes, stirring occasionally. Mix together in a bowl the breadcrumbs, prunes, nuts and herbs and stir in the onion. Season with nutmeg, salt and pepper and beat in the egg. Divide the mixture between the peppers and place them in a greased baking dish. Beat together the yoghurt and egg and season with salt and pepper. Spoon the topping over the peppers.

Bake in a pre-heated oven, 190°C (375°F), Gas 5, for 40 minutes. Serve hot.

Serves 4

SWEETCORN PEPPERS

4 large green or red peppers
salt
450 g (1 lb) frozen sweetcorn kernels
60 ml (4 tablespoons) vegetable stock (page 12)
50 g (2 oz) butter
30 ml (2 tablespoons) dried milk powder
30 ml (2 tablespoons) double cream
5 ml (1 teaspoon) lemon juice
30 ml (2 tablespoons) chopped fresh parsley
2 eggs, separated
pepper
60 ml (4 tablespoons) grated cheese

Cut the stalks from the peppers and cut a very thin slice from one side. Scoop out the seeds and pith. Blanch the peppers in boiling salted water for 10 minutes, then drain and pat them dry.

Simmer the sweetcorn with the stock and butter for 10 minutes, or until it is tender. Liquidize in a blender, then blend in the milk powder, cream and lemon juice. Turn the purée into a bowl and beat in the parsley and egg yolks. Season with salt and pepper. Whisk the egg whites until they are stiff. Fold them into the purée. Place the pepper shells in a greased baking dish and spoon the purée into them. Sprinkle on the cheese.

Bake in a pre-heated oven, 190°C (375°F), Gas 5, for 25 minutes, or until the filling is well risen and set. Serve at once.

Serves 4

* Boiled rice, wholewheat grains or millet seeds and a green salad would go well with this dish.
* As an alternative, make a pea purée filling for red peppers, using 600 g (1¼ lb) shelled or frozen peas. Season the purée with chopped mint and a pinch of grated nutmeg.
* Or use carrot purée, great with yellow or green peppers. Use 750 g (1½ lb) carrots, seasoned with mint.

JACKET POTATOES

Almost a meal in themselves, with tasty additions of chopped vegetables, cheese or nuts; or 'handy' fillers to serve with other dishes – where would we be without them?

    4 large potatoes, scrubbed
    40 g (1½ oz) butter
    90 ml (6 tablespoons) blanched almonds, flaked
    60 ml (4 tablespoons) double cream
    30 ml (2 tablespoons) chopped fresh parsley
    90 ml (6 tablespoons) cheese, grated
    salt and pepper

Dry the potatoes and prick them with a fork to prevent the skins from bursting. Bake them in a pre-heated oven, 190°C (375°F), Gas 5, for 1-1¼ hours, or until they are soft.

Melt 15 g (½ oz) of the butter in a pan and fry the almonds until they are a deep golden brown.

Cut a thin slice from the top of each potato. Use a dessert-spoon to scoop out the centre, taking care not to pierce the skin. Mash the potato with the remaining butter. Beat in the almonds, cream, parsley and 30 ml (2 tablespoons) of the cheese. Season with salt and pepper. Pile the potato mixture back into the skins, place the potatoes on the grill rack and sprinkle on the remaining cheese. Cook under the grill, pre-heated to high, for 5 minutes. Serve hot.

Serves 4

* Think laterally – mix the potato with finely diced cooked carrots, sesame seeds and cheese; chopped chives, a little vegetable purée (parsnip is good) and cottage cheese; chopped cooked spinach, nutmeg and soured cream. Yesterday's over-catering (or planning ahead) is today's potato variety.

BAKED TOMATOES

    8 large tomatoes
    30 ml (2 tablespoons) oil
    1 large onion, peeled and finely chopped
    1 clove garlic, peeled and crushed
    100 g (4 oz) mushrooms, chopped
    75 g (3 oz) cheese, grated
    50 g (2 oz) chopped walnuts
    60 ml (4 tablespoons) wholewheat breadcrumbs
    15 ml (1 tablespoon) chopped chives
    15 ml (1 tablespoon) chopped fresh parsley
    1 egg, beaten
    salt and pepper

Cut a thin slice from the top of each tomato. Using a teaspoon, scoop out the seeds and flesh, taking care not to pierce the skin.

Heat the oil in a pan and fry the onion and garlic over moderate heat for 3 minutes, stirring once or twice. Stir in the mushrooms and tomato seeds and flesh and cook for 2 minutes. Remove from the heat and beat in the cheese, walnuts, breadcrumbs, herbs and egg and season well with salt and pepper. Place the tomato cases in a greased baking dish and pile in the filling.

Cook in a pre-heated oven, 200°C (400°F), Gas 6, for 20 minutes. Serve hot with, perhaps, rice or wholewheat grains. *Serves 4*

VINE-LEAF PARCELS

A golden filling of dried apricots, sultanas and rice makes an imaginative vegetarian version of the traditional Greek *dolmathes*. A crisp salad of endive, watercress and orange segments and lots of hot crusty bread go well.

450-g (1-lb) jar vine leaves
30 ml (2 tablespoons) oil
1 small onion, peeled and finely chopped
1 clove garlic, peeled and crushed
75 g (3 oz) brown rice
50 g (2 oz) sultanas
100 g (4 oz) dried apricots, finely chopped
10 ml (2 teaspoons) chopped fresh mint
5 ml (1 teaspoon) grated lemon rind
10 ml (2 teaspoons) lemon juice
300 ml (½ pint) vegetable stock (page 12)
a pinch of ground coriander
salt and pepper

For the sauce
300 ml (½ pint) vegetable stock (page 12)
150 ml (¼ pint) unsweetened pineapple juice
10 ml (2 teaspoons) lemon juice

For garnish
90 ml (6 tablespoons) plain yoghurt

Drain and unroll the vine leaves. Use 10–12 to cover a shallow, greased baking dish.

Heat the oil in a frying-pan and cook the onion and garlic over moderate heat for 2 minutes. Stir in the rice, then add the sultanas, apricots, mint, lemon rind, lemon juice and stock. Season with the coriander, salt and pepper and bring to the boil. Lower the heat, cover the pan and simmer for 40 minutes, until the rice is just tender. Taste and adjust the seasoning if needed. Allow to cool.

Spoon a heaped teaspoon of the filling on to the centre of each of 36 vine leaves. Fold up the stalk end almost to cover the filling, fold both sides to the middle, then roll up from the stalk end to make tight parcels. Arrange the filled leaves, seam sides down, in the dish. Mix together the stock, pineapple and lemon juice and pour over the parcels. Cover completely with more vine leaves and then with foil.

Cook in a pre-heated oven, 170°C (325°F), Gas 3, for 50 minutes. Remove the covering leaves and swirl on the yoghurt. Serve hot or cold.
Serves 6

CABBAGE SALAD BOWL

1 medium firm white cabbage
4 dessert apples, cored and diced
100 g (4 oz) Cheddar cheese, diced
225 g (8 oz) walnut halves
50 g (2 oz) sultanas

For the dressing
75 ml (5 tablespoons) oil

15 ml (1 tablespoon) cider vinegar
15 ml (1 tablespoon) clear honey
50 g (2 oz) Stilton, crumbled
pepper

Discard the discoloured outer leaves of the cabbage and trim it neatly. Pull apart the centre and cut away the inner leaves, leaving 2.5-cm (1-in)-thick 'walls'. Shred the cabbage centre finely and mix with the apples, cheese, walnuts and sultanas.

Liquidize the dressing ingredients in a blender. Toss the cabbage salad in the dressing and pile it into the cabbage shell.

Serves 8

CHILLED COURGETTES

Serve them as an interesting first course or as part of a cold 'mains' selection, drawing on a stock of ready-cooked grains or vegetables.

8 medium courgettes
salt
45 ml (3 tablespoons) oil
100 g (4 oz) mushrooms, chopped
4 tomatoes, skinned and chopped
100 g (4 oz) cooked wholewheat grains
50 g (2 oz) cooked brown rice
15 ml (1 tablespoon) red wine vinegar
5 ml (1 teaspoon) lemon juice
15 ml (1 tablespoon) chopped fresh parsley
5 ml (1 teaspoon) chopped chives
15 ml (1 tablespoon) sunflower seeds
pepper

Blanch the courgettes in boiling, salted water for 6 minutes, drain and dry them. Cut them in half lengthways and scoop out the flesh with a teaspoon, leaving firm walls. Chop the flesh. Heat the oil in a pan and fry the mushrooms and chopped courgettes over moderate heat for 2 minutes; add the tomatoes, stir and cook for 3 minutes more. Mix the vegetables with the wheat and rice then stir in the vinegar, lemon juice, herbs and sunflower seeds. Season with salt and pepper.

Pile the filling into the courgette shells, cool and chill. *Serves 4*

* As an alternative, substitute 100 g (4 oz) cooked small cauliflower florets and 75 g (3 oz) cooked red kidney beans for the wheat and mushrooms. The result – a colourful, crunchy salad blend.

POPEYE TOMATOES

Lovely to look at, they make an eye-catching 'opener' or can decorate a main dish.

8 large tomatoes
90 ml (6 tablespoons) vinaigrette dressing (page 54)
450 g (1 lb) spinach
salt
60 ml (4 tablespoons) blanched almonds
pepper
1 small onion, peeled and finely chopped
2 hard-boiled eggs

Cut a cross through the top of each tomato to the base, but without actually cutting it into quarters. Pour on the dressing and set aside for 1 hour, spooning the dressing over the tomatoes occasionally.

Strip the stalks from the spinach and cook the leaves in boiling, salted water for about 3 minutes, just until they collapse. Drain the leaves and press out all excess moisture. Chop the leaves, toss them with the almonds and 60 ml (4 tablespoons) of the dressing and season with salt and pepper. Chop one hard-boiled egg and mix it with the onion. Slice the other.

Spoon the spinach into the tomatoes so they look like opened-out water lilies. Scatter the onion and egg mixture on top and garnish each tomato with an egg slice.

Serves 4–8

7 Other Main Dishes

After salads, rice and other grain dishes, pasta, pastry flans, pies and pasties, and filled-to-the-brim vegetables, what other 'main' dishes are there? Answer – too many to fit into one chapter!

First, there are baked vegetable dishes with a whole range of toppings – crisped-up crumbs, cheesy crumbles, scone-dough cobbler, and good old mashed potato. There are pancakes, some with built-in fibre-plus in the form of chopped spinach, with spiced or creamy vegetable fillings. There are terrines to be enjoyed hot or cold, as a snack or part of a pretty elaborate buffet meal. Of course there are pulse dishes, as varied as baked lentil roll, red-hot peppery bean goulash, and dried bean hotpot. Pizza with whole-wheat flour and high-in-fibre mushroom topping comes well within our terms of reference, and so does a vegetable soufflé when the main ingredient is spinach.

Again, follow the golden fibre rule. Look for every opportunity in your every-day cooking to add pulses, seeds and nuts. A handful of dried beans in a vegetable hotpot, ground walnuts or sesame seeds in a crumble topping, toasted almonds scattered atop curried vegetables, all add that valuable extra touch of fibre – and delicious texture, too.

ARTICHOKES AU GRATIN

450 g (1 lb) Jerusalem artichokes, well scrubbed
15 ml (1 tablespoon) lemon juice
salt
40 g (1½ oz) margarine
1 medium onion, peeled and sliced
2 leeks, well washed and sliced into thin rings
100 g (4 oz) button mushrooms, sliced
10 ml (2 teaspoons) grated orange rind
15 ml (1 tablespoon) wholewheat flour
75 ml (5 tablespoons) vegetable stock (page 12)
150 ml (¼ pint) single cream
salt and pepper

For the topping
50 g (2 oz) wholewheat breadcrumbs
60 ml (4 tablespoons) sunflower seeds
75 g (3 oz) Cheddar cheese, grated
25 g (1 oz) rolled porage oats

Dice the artichokes straight into a pan of water and add the lemon juice – otherwise they go an unappetizing brown colour. Add salt, bring to the boil, cover and cook for 5 minutes. Drain.

Melt the margarine in a pan and fry the onion and leeks over moderate heat for 2–4 minutes, stirring once or twice. Stir in the artichokes, cook for 2 minutes, then add the mushrooms and orange rind and cook for a further minute. Stir in the flour and pour on the stock and the cream. Bring just to the boil, stirring. Season with salt and pepper and turn the vegetables into a pie dish.

Mix together in a bowl the breadcrumbs, seeds, cheese and oats and sprinkle the mixture over the vegetables. Bake in a pre-heated oven, 190°C (375°F), Gas 5, for 30 minutes, or until the cheese is brown and bubbling.
Serves 4

BEAN GOULASH

225 g (8 oz) soya beans, soaked and drained
45 ml (3 tablespoons) oil
2 medium onions, peeled and sliced
4 stalks celery, thinly sliced
2 cloves garlic, peeled and crushed
15 ml (1 tablespoon) paprika
10 ml (2 tablespoons) caraway seeds
15 ml (1 tablespoon) tomato purée
150 ml (¼ pint) vegetable stock (page 12)
400-g (14-oz) can tomatoes
30 ml (2 tablespoons) chopped fresh parsley
2 bay leaves
salt and pepper
100 g (4 oz) button mushrooms, sliced

For garnish
60 ml (4 tablespoons) soured cream

Cook the beans in boiling, unsalted water for 3 hours, or until they are tender, then drain. Heat the oil in a flameproof casserole, fry the onions, celery and garlic over moderate heat for 3–4 minutes, stirring once or twice. Stir in the paprika and caraway seeds, cook for 1 minute then add the tomato purée, stock and tomatoes. Add the parsley, bay leaves and beans and season with salt and pepper. Bring to the boil, cover and cook in a pre-heated oven, 180°C (350°F), Gas 5, for 1 hour. Stir in the mushrooms, adjust the seasoning if necessary, and cook for 15 minutes more. Discard the bay leaves. Swirl with the soured cream and serve.

Serves 4

BROCCOLI SEEDS BAKE

450 g (1 lb) broccoli spears
3 medium onions, peeled and chopped
salt
25 g (1 oz) margarine
30 ml (2 tablespoons) wholewheat flour
225 ml (8 fl oz) milk
75 g (3 oz) cream cheese
60 ml (4 tablespoons) pumpkin seeds
pepper
100 g (4 oz) Cheddar cheese, grated

For the topping
40 g (1½ oz) butter
75 g (3 oz) wholewheat breadcrumbs
30 ml (2 tablespoons) chopped fresh parsley
45 ml (3 tablespoons) sunflower seeds

Steam the broccoli and onion over boiling, salted water until just tender. Melt the margarine in a pan, stir in the flour and when it forms a roux, gradually pour on the milk, stirring. Bring to the boil, stirring, then simmer for 3 minutes. Beat in the cream cheese and pumpkin seeds and season with salt and pepper. Mix the broccoli and onion into the sauce and pour into a pie dish. Cover with the grated cheese.

To make the topping, melt the butter and stir in the breadcrumbs, parsley and sunflower seeds. Spread over the cheese layer.

Bake in a pre-heated oven, 180°C (350°F), Gas 4, for 30–35 minutes, or until the top is crisp. Serve hot.
Serves 4

* Baked tomatoes, sprinkled with herbs and cooked in the oven at the same time, go well.

CHEESE AND HERB COBBLER

225 g (8 oz) cauliflower, cut into florets
225 g (8 oz) carrots
225 g (8 oz) parsnips
1 head celery, sliced
salt
100 g (4 oz) button mushrooms, sliced
225 g (8 oz) cream cheese
pepper

For the topping
225 g (8 oz) wholewheat flour
5 ml (1 teaspoon) bicarbonate of soda
2.5 ml (½ teaspoon) mustard powder
50 g (2 oz) butter
5 ml (1 teaspoon) mixed dried herbs
150 ml (¼ pint) plain yoghurt
milk, for glazing

Steam the cauliflower, carrots, parsnips and celery over boiling, salted water until they are just tender. Reserve the liquid. Dice the root vegetables and mix all with the mushrooms. Beat 45–60 ml (3–4 tablespoons) of the cooking liquid into the cream cheese, season with salt and pepper and stir it into the vegetables. Turn the mixture into a pie dish.

To make the scone topping, sift together the flour, soda, mustard and salt and tip in the bran from the sieve. Rub in the butter until the mixture is crumb-like, stir in the herbs and then the yoghurt. Mix to a firm dough. Roll out on a lightly-floured board to 12-mm (½-in) thickness. Cut into rounds with a 5-cm (2-in) cutter. Arrange the scone rings over the vegetables and brush the tops with milk.

Bake in a pre-heated oven, 220°C (425°F), Gas 7, for 10 minutes. Reduce the heat to 200°C (400°F), Gas 6, and

continue cooking for 15 minutes, or until the scone topping is well risen and golden brown. Serve hot.
Serves 4-6

CREAMY CURRIED VEGETABLES

1 small cauliflower, cut into florets
225 g (8 oz) carrots, diced
225 g (8 oz) French beans, topped and tailed and cut into 5-cm (2-in) slices
450 g (1 lb) broad beans, shelled (or use 225 g (8 oz) frozen beans, thawed)
salt
45 ml (3 tablespoons) oil
1 medium onion, peeled and sliced
2 cloves garlic, peeled and crushed
15 ml (1 tablespoon) garam masala
5 ml (1 teaspoon) paprika
2.5 ml (½ teaspoon) cayenne pepper (optional)
15 ml (1 tablespoon) wholewheat flour
75 ml (5 tablespoons) double cream
30 ml (2 tablespoons) chopped fresh coriander leaves, or parsley

For garnish
60 ml (4 tablespoons) blanched almonds, toasted

Steam the vegetables over boiling, salted water until they are just tender. Reserve the liquid.

Heat the oil in a pan and fry the onion and garlic over moderate heat for 3-4 minutes. Stir in the spices and cook for 1 minute, then add the flour. When it forms a roux pour on 300 ml (½ pint) of the reserved vegetable liquid, stirring until the sauce thickens. Stir in the cream and then the vegetables and the chopped coriander. Allow all the ingredients to heat through and the flavours to blend for 5 minutes over very low heat.

Serve hot, sprinkled with the almonds, on a bed of brown rice.

Serves 4

* Lovely hot, floppy pieces of *Nan* make a perfect 'extra' to this and other spicy dishes. You can make them quickly and easily from a packet mix – pretty well foolproof.

HARICOT HOTPOT

225 g (8 oz) dried haricot beans, soaked and drained
a few parsley stalks
2 bay leaves
25 g (1 oz) margarine
4 stalks celery, sliced
2 medium onions, peeled and sliced
225 g (8 oz) carrots, thickly sliced
225 g (8 oz) parsnips, diced
425 ml (¾ pint) vegetable stock (page 12)
5 ml (1 teaspoon) yeast extract
30 ml (2 tablespoons) chopped fresh parsley
salt and pepper
100 g (4 oz) button mushrooms

Cook the beans in unsalted water flavoured with the parsley stalks, bay leaves and a few celery stalks for about 1¼ hours, or until they are tender. Drain them and discard the herbs.

Melt the margarine in a flameproof casserole and fry the celery and onion over moderate heat for 4–5 minutes. Add the carrots, parsnips, stock, yeast extract, beans and parsley and season with salt and pepper. Cover the casserole and bake in a pre-heated oven, 180°C (350°F), Gas 4, for 1¼

hours. Stir in the mushrooms, adjust the seasoning if necessary and cook for a further 15 minutes.
Serves 4

* Cubes of Cheddar cheese stirred in with the mushrooms are a tasty way of adding dairy protein. Another is to top the casserole with thin slices of French bread thickly covered with grated cheese and browned under the grill.

MIXED PLATTER WITH PEANUT SAUCE

    450 g (1 lb) carrots, quartered lengthways
    6 courgettes, thickly sliced
    8 stalks celery, cut into 5-cm (2-in) slices
    350 g (12 oz) small new potatoes, scrubbed
    salt
    4 hard-boiled eggs, quartered

    For the sauce
    10 ml (2 teaspoons) oil
    175 g (6 oz) raw peanuts
    1 large onion, peeled and sliced
    2 cloves garlic, peeled
    5 ml (1 teaspoon) cayenne
    15 ml (1 tablespoon) dark Muscovado sugar
    300 ml (½ pint) water
    salt

Steam the vegetables over boiling, salted water until they are just tender. While they are cooking, make the sauce. Heat the oil in a pan and fry the peanuts over moderate heat, stirring frequently, for 5 minutes. Leave the nuts to cool a little then liquidize in a blender with the onion and garlic. Add the cayenne, sugar and water and blend to make a smooth sauce. Season with salt.

Arrange the hot, cooked vegetables and egg slices on a dish and serve the sauce separately.

Serves 4

* Rice and pitta bread are good accompaniments.

MUSHROOM AND WALNUT PÂTÉ

Serve it as a first course with fingers of hot wholewheat toast, or as a light meal with salad.

75 g (3 oz) butter
2 medium onions, peeled and finely chopped
450 g (1 lb) mushrooms, finely chopped
5 ml (1 teaspoon) dried basil
60 ml (4 tablespoons) chopped fresh parsley
150 ml (¼ pint) red wine
150 ml (¼ pint) vegetable stock (page 12)
5 ml (1 teaspoon) yeast extract
salt and pepper
75 ml (5 tablespoons) double cream
75 g (3 oz) chopped walnuts

For decoration
a few walnut halves

Melt the butter in a pan and fry the onions over moderate heat for 3 minutes. Stir in the mushrooms, basil, half the parsley, wine, stock and yeast extract and season with salt and pepper. Cover and simmer for 45 minutes. Beat well, increase the heat and cook uncovered for 15–20 minutes, until the mixture is thick and the liquid has evaporated. Leave to cool, then beat in the cream and walnuts and remaining parsley. Turn into a bowl and level the top. Decorate with walnut halves. Cover and chill before serving.

Serves 6

POTATO PIE

25 g (1 oz) margarine
2 medium onions, peeled and sliced
4 stalks celery, thinly sliced
1 bulb fennel, thinly sliced
2 medium carrots, grated
10 ml (2 teaspoons) wholewheat flour
150 ml (¼ pint) vegetable stock (page 12)
30 ml (2 tablespoons) chopped fresh parsley
salt and pepper
75 g (3 oz) Cheddar cheese, grated

For the topping
450 g (1 lb) potatoes, cooked and mashed
2 eggs, separated
salt and pepper

Melt the margarine in a pan and fry the onions, celery and fennel over moderately low heat for 10 minutes, stirring once or twice. Stir in the carrots and the flour, increase the heat and pour on the stock. Stir in the parsley and season with salt and pepper. Simmer for 5 minutes.

Pour half the vegetable mixture into a pie dish, spread with 50 g (2 oz) of the cheese and cover with the remaining vegetables.

Beat the egg yolks and the remaining cheese into the potatoes and season with salt and pepper. Stiffly whisk the egg whites and fold them into the potato. Spread the mixture over the vegetables.

Bake the pie in a pre-heated oven, 200°C (400°F), Gas 6, for 35–40 minutes, or until the topping is well risen and brown. Serve hot.
Serves 4

RATATOUILLE

2 aubergines, diced
salt
about 120 ml (8 tablespoons) olive oil
1 large onion, peeled and sliced
2 cloves garlic, peeled and crushed
1 green pepper, seeded and sliced
1 red pepper, seeded and sliced
4 courgettes, thickly sliced
225 g (8 oz) tomatoes, skinned and chopped
30 ml (2 tablespoons) chopped fresh parsley
5 ml (1 teaspoon) dried oregano
pepper
100 g (4 oz) cooked dried haricot beans

Put the aubergines into a colander, sprinkle with salt and leave to drain for 30 minutes. Rinse under cold water and pat dry.

Heat 30 ml (2 tablespoons) of the oil in a frying-pan and fry the onion and garlic over moderate heat for 3–4 minutes, stirring once or twice. Add the green and red peppers, fry for 3 minutes. Transfer the cooked vegetables to a flameproof casserole and set aside.

Add more oil to the pan, fry the courgettes for 4–5 minutes, transfer them to the casserole. Add more oil to the pan and fry the aubergines in 2 or 3 batches, then add them to the casserole with the tomatoes and herbs; season well with salt and pepper. Cover the casserole and simmer for 20 minutes. Stir in the beans and simmer for 10 minutes more. Taste and add more seasoning if needed.

Serve hot, with rice; or cold as a first course – this way, it's delicious with garlic- and herb-flavoured cream cheese.
Serves 4–6

SPINACH SOUFFLÉ

225-g (8-oz) packet frozen spinach, thawed and chopped
50 g (2 oz) butter
45 ml (3 tablespoons) wholewheat flour
200 ml (7 fl oz) milk
5 ml (1 teaspoon) lemon juice
salt and pepper
3 eggs, separated
1 egg white
100 g (4 oz) Emmenthal cheese, grated
60 ml (4 tablespoons) wholewheat breadcrumbs
45 ml (3 tablespoons) chopped walnuts

Press out all the moisture from the spinach and put it in a non-stick pan over low heat for a minute or two.

Melt the butter in another pan, stir in the flour and when it forms a roux gradually pour on the milk, stirring. Bring to the boil, stirring all the time, add the spinach and lemon juice and season with salt and pepper. Beat well and simmer for 2–3 minutes then remove from the heat and cool slightly. Beat in the egg yolks and 75 g (3 oz) of the cheese. Stiffly whisk the egg whites and fold them into the mixture.

Turn the mixture into a greased 1.1-litre (2-pint) soufflé dish. Mix together the remaining cheese, the breadcrumbs and walnuts and sprinkle on the top.

Bake in a pre-heated oven, 190°C (375°F), Gas 5, for 30–35 minutes, or until the soufflé is just set. It is very important to serve it at once, before it collapses.

Serves 4

* Vegetable soufflés offer lots of opportunity for originality. Try using 300 ml (½ pint) of thick vegetable purée in place of the spinach – carrot with a dash of grated orange rind is good; green pea and mint (blended together in the

liquidizer), or Jerusalem artichoke with orange, are other successes.

VEGETABLE CASSEROLE

50 g (2 oz) margarine
225 g (8 oz) small onions or shallots, peeled
1 clove garlic, peeled and crushed
350 g (12 oz) carrots, thickly sliced
225 g (8 oz) potatoes, diced
225 g (8 oz) parsnips, diced
4 courgettes, thickly sliced
300 ml ($\frac{1}{2}$ pint) vegetable stock (page 12), hot
5 ml (1 teaspoon) yeast extract
5 ml (1 teaspoon) tomato purée
5 ml (1 teaspoon) dried oregano
2.5 ml ($\frac{1}{2}$ teaspoon) dried basil
salt and pepper
100 g (4 oz) small button mushrooms (slice large ones)
30 ml (2 tablespoons) chopped fresh parsley

For serving (optional)
90 ml (6 tablespoons) croûtons (page 30)

Melt the margarine in a flameproof casserole and fry the whole onions for 5 minutes over moderate heat, stirring occasionally. Add the garlic, carrots, potatoes and parsnips and cook, stirring once or twice, for 5 minutes more. Add the courgettes and stir well.

Stir together the stock, yeast extract and tomato purée and pour over the vegetables. Add the herbs and season with salt and pepper. Cover and simmer for 5 minutes, stirring once or twice. Add the mushrooms and continue cooking for 5 minutes, or until all the vegetables are just tender. Stir in the parsley, taste and adjust the seasoning. Scatter with the croûtons, if using, just before serving.

Serves 4

VEGETABLE CRUMBLE

25 g (1 oz) margarine
2 large onions, peeled and sliced
2 stalks celery, sliced
450 g (1 lb) carrots, diced
225 g (8 oz) parsnips, diced
225 g (8 oz) white turnips, diced
425 ml (¾ pint) vegetable stock (page 12)
5 ml (1 teaspoon) yeast extract
15 ml (1 tablespoon) tomato purée
salt and pepper
350 g (12 oz) broccoli spears, or cauliflower florets
30 ml (2 tablespoons) chopped fresh parsley

For the topping
75 g (3 oz) margarine
75 g (3 oz) wholewheat flour
5 ml (1 teaspoon) ground coriander
50 g (2 oz) chopped walnuts
30 ml (2 tablespoons) sesame seeds
salt and pepper

Melt the margarine in a pan and fry the onions and celery over moderate heat for 3–4 minutes, stirring once or twice. Add the carrots, parsnips and turnips, the stock, yeast extract and tomato purée and season with salt and pepper. Bring to the boil, cover and simmer for 10 minutes. Stir in the broccoli or cauliflower and the parsley, return to the boil and simmer for 5 minutes more.

For the topping, rub the margarine into the flour and stir in the coriander, walnuts and seeds. Season with salt and pepper.

Turn the vegetables into a pie dish and leave to cool. (You can make the dish to this stage in advance, like overnight.)

Sprinkle on the crumble topping and bake in a pre-heated oven, 190°C (375°F), Gas 5, for 25–30 minutes, or until the topping is crisp. Serve hot.

Serves 4

VEGETABLE TERRINE

An elegant cold dish to serve as the centrepiece of a salad meal.

> 350 g (12 oz) French beans, topped and tailed
> 450 g (1 lb) broad beans, shelled (or use 225 g (8 oz) frozen beans, thawed)
> 350 g (12 oz) young carrots
> salt
> 10 ml (2 teaspoons) agar-agar
> 30 ml (2 tablespoons) orange juice
> 275 g (10 oz) mayonnaise
> 30 ml (2 tablespoons) soured cream
> 5 ml (1 teaspoon) grated orange rind
> pepper

> *For garnish*
> orange slices

Cook the beans, broad beans and carrots in boiling, salted water until they are just tender. Drain and dry them. Cut the French beans into 5-cm (2-in) slices and the carrots into matchstick strips.

Stir the agar-agar into the orange juice, heat gently to

dissolve, and leave to cool. Mix together the mayonnaise, soured cream and orange rind. When the orange juice is cool, stir it into the mayonnaise and season well with pepper.

Line an 18-cm (7-in) cake tin with non-stick silicone paper. Spread a thin layer of mayonnaise in the base and arrange a layer of French beans. Cover with mayonnaise and then carrots, mayonnaise and then broad beans. Cover with the remaining mayonnaise.

Cover the tin and chill for 2 hours. Invert the mould on to a serving dish and garnish with slices of orange.

Serves 6

FRUIT AND VEGETABLE KEBABS

Vary the vegetables and fruit combination – including, for example, sliced peppers, sections of whole sweetcorn, and apple wedges.

1 large aubergine, halved and cut into 2.5-cm (1-in) slices
2 medium courgettes, cut into 2.5-cm (1-in) slices
salt
100 g (4 oz) button mushrooms
8 small onions or shallots, peeled
12 dried apricots, soaked and drained
2 bananas, thickly sliced

For the marinade
30 ml (2 tablespoons) cider vinegar
75 ml (5 tablespoons) olive oil
5 ml (1 teaspoon) grated lemon rind
5 ml (1 teaspoon) lemon juice
salt and pepper

Put the aubergine and courgette slices into a colander,

sprinkle them with salt and leave to drain for 30 minutes. Rinse under cold, running water, drain and pat dry.

Thread the vegetables and fruit on to 4 greased kebab sticks. Mix together the marinade ingredients and brush the kebabs to coat them well. Set aside for 30 minutes or so.

Brush the kebabs with the remaining dressing. Cook them under a grill heated to high for 6–8 minutes, turning them once.

Serves 4

* Serve with brown rice tossed with sweetcorn and toasted almonds.

CHICK-PEA CAKES

Known as Felafel in the Middle East, these fibre-full pulse 'cakes' are usually served with hot pitta bread and salad.

275 g (10 oz) dried chick-peas, soaked and drained
2 large onions, peeled and chopped
2 cloves garlic, peeled
45 ml (3 tablespoons) lemon juice
2.5 ml ($\frac{1}{2}$ teaspoon) cayenne pepper
5 ml (1 teaspoon) ground coriander
5 ml (1 teaspoon) ground cumin
salt
oil, for deep frying

For garnish
sprigs of mint

For serving
1 lemon, quartered

Cook the chick-peas in boiling, unsalted water for about $2\frac{1}{2}$ hours, or until they are tender. Liquidize them in a blender with the onions, garlic and lemon juice. Alternatively mash the peas, finely chop the onions, crush the garlic and mix together. Beat in the spices and season with salt. Cover and chill for 30 minutes.

Shape the mixture into small flat 'cakes'. Heat the oil in a pan to 190°C (375°F), or until a cube of day-old bread browns in 50 seconds. Fry the cakes until they are golden brown. Drain on kitchen paper, garnish with mint and serve with lemon wedges.

Serves 4

LENTIL ROLL

    350 g (12 oz) red lentils, washed and drained
    450 ml (¾ pint) water
    40 g (1½ oz) margarine
    1 large onion, peeled and finely chopped
    7.5 ml (1½ teaspoons) curry powder
    15 ml (1 tablespoon) chopped fresh parsley
    1 egg, beaten
    60 ml (4 tablespoons) finely chopped walnuts
    salt and pepper
    flour, for dusting
    90 ml (6 tablespoons) oil
    4 medium onions, peeled
    5 ml (1 teaspoon) dried thyme

Cook the lentils in unsalted water for 30 minutes, or until they are tender. Beat them well and continue cooking, uncovered, to evaporate any remaining liquid. Beat well to form a smooth purée. Leave to cool.

Melt the margarine in a pan and fry the onion over moderate heat for 4–5 minutes, stirring occasionally. Stir in the curry powder and cook for 1 minute more. Beat the onion mixture into the lentils with the egg and walnuts and season well with salt and pepper. On a lightly-floured board, shape the paste into a roll about the size of a 450-g (1-lb) can. Dust the roll all over with flour.

Heat the oil in a roasting pan. Sprinkle the onions with the dried thyme. Place the lentil roll and the onions in the roasting pan and cook in a pre-heated oven, 190°C (375°F), Gas 5, for 50 minutes, turning the roll to brown it evenly. *Serves 4–6*

* Serve with Tomato sauce (page 261) or Sweet and sour sauce (page 260). Baked or steamed courgettes go especially well.

WATERCRESS CUTLETS

50 g (2 oz) butter
50 g (2 oz) wholewheat flour, plus extra for coating
200 ml (7 fl oz) milk
4 hard-boiled eggs, chopped
salt and pepper
a pinch of cayenne
1 bunch watercress, trimmed and chopped
1 large egg, beaten
75 g (3 oz) ground hazelnuts
25 g (1 oz) wholewheat breadcrumbs
oil or butter, for frying

For serving
1 lemon, quartered

Melt the butter in a pan, stir in the flour and when it forms a roux, gradually pour on the milk, stirring. Bring to the boil, stirring all the time. Remove from the heat and beat the sauce until it is smooth and glossy. Leave to cool a little. Stir

in the chopped eggs and season with salt, pepper and
cayenne. Stir in the watercress.

Flour your hands and shape the paste into 8 flat 'cakes'.
Dip them in flour, then in beaten egg, then in a mixture of
the ground nuts and breadcrumbs.

Fry the cutlets in the oil or butter for 4-5 minutes on each
side until they are golden brown. Serve hot with a wedge of
lemon.

Serves 4

* A salad of watercress sprigs, fennel and orange segments
goes especially well.

VEGETABLE FRITTERS

1 small aubergine, cut into 12-mm ($\frac{1}{2}$-in) slices
salt
1 small cauliflower, cut into florets
100 g (4 oz) button mushrooms, trimmed
oil, for deep frying

For the batter
175 ml (6 fl oz) milk
1 egg, separated
15 ml (1 tablespoon) oil
125 g (5 oz) wholewheat flour

For serving
Sweet and sour sauce (page 260)

Put the aubergine slices in a colander, sprinkle with salt and
leave to drain for 30 minutes. Rinse under a cold tap and
pat dry. Steam the cauliflower over boiling, salted water for
10 minutes, plunge into cold water and pat dry.

To make the batter, put the milk, egg yolk, oil and flour
in a blender, add salt and whizz. Leave to stand for 30
minutes. Stiffly whisk the egg white and fold into the batter.

Heat the oil for deep frying. Dip the vegetables into the batter and drain off excess. When the oil reaches 190°C (375°F) fry a batch of the vegetables for 4–5 minutes, or until they are crisp and golden. Drain the cooked vegetables on crumpled kitchen paper and keep them warm. When the oil returns to the original temperature, fry the next batch.

Serve the fritters hot, with rice and the sweet and sour sauce.

Serves 4

* No time to make the sauce? Stir 100 g (4 oz) grated cheese into the batter after folding in the egg white and proceed as described. Cheesy fritters are marvellous!

BEANSPROUTS FOO YUNG

45 ml (3 tablespoons) sesame or peanut oil
1 piece ginger root, peeled and finely chopped
2 spring onions, peeled and thinly sliced
100 g (4 oz) fresh beansprouts, or use canned ones, rinsed and drained
50 g (2 oz) mushrooms, chopped
50 g (2 oz) blanched almonds, flaked
30 ml (2 tablespoons) sherry
15 ml (1 tablespoon) soy sauce
6 eggs, well beaten

Heat 30 ml (2 tablespoons) of the oil in a pan. Stir-fry the ginger over high heat for 1 minute. Add the onion, beansprouts, mushrooms and almonds. Stir well and pour on the sherry and soy sauce. Bring to the boil and beat into the egg mixture.

Heat the remaining oil in an 18-cm (7-in) omelette pan. Pour in one quarter of the egg mixture, stir well and cook for 1–2 minutes until the underside is brown. Turn the omelette on to a large plate and slide it back into the pan to cook the other side. Cook for 1-2 minutes, until evenly brown. Set aside to keep warm. Cook 3 more omelettes in the same way, heating a little more oil if necessary.

Serve the omelettes hot, folded in half.

Serves 4

* Brown rice and Sweet and sour sauce (page 260) are good accompaniments.

BROCCOLI PANCAKES WITH LEMON SAUCE

These tiny pancakes the size of small drop scones are appetizing and light.

> 450 g (1 lb) broccoli spears
> 1 medium onion, peeled and quartered
> salt
> 4 large eggs
> 25 g (1 oz) wholewheat flour
> pepper
> butter, for frying

> *For the sauce*
> 15 ml (1 tablespoon) lemon juice
> 15 ml (1 tablespoon) water
> 5 ml (1 teaspoon) cider vinegar
> 4 peppercorns
> 4 egg yolks
> 225 g (8 oz) butter, diced

> *For serving*
> 1 lemon, quartered

Steam the broccoli and onion over boiling, salted water for 10 minutes, or until it is just tender, then chop it roughly.

Whizz the eggs, broccoli, onion, flour, pepper and salt

for a few seconds in a blender until the vegetables are chopped but not liquidized. Set aside.

To make the sauce, put the lemon juice, water and vinegar in a pan with the peppercorns. Bring to the boil and cook until 15 ml (1 tablespoon) liquid remains. Strain into the top of a double boiler or a bowl fitted over a pan of simmering water. Whisk in the egg yolks and then the butter a little at a time. Continue beating until all the butter has melted and the sauce has thickened. Cover closely with a piece of wetted greaseproof paper.

Heat a large pan over moderate heat, grease it with butter and drop 30 ml (2 tablespoons) portions of the mixture well apart. Cook for 2–3 minutes until the undersides are brown, flip over and cook the second sides. Keep the first batch warm while you cook the remaining pancakes.

Serve the pancakes hot with the lemon slices and the hot sauce.

Serves 4

* There'll be sauce to spare for spooning on to an accompanying vegetable – spinach or asparagus go well.

CURRIED VEGETABLE PANCAKES

300 ml (½ pint) milk
1 egg
1 egg yolk
100 g (4 oz) wholewheat flour
salt
oil, for frying

For the filling
450 g (1 lb) potatoes, scrubbed and sliced
10 ml (2 teaspoons) ground turmeric

30 ml (2 tablespoons) peanut oil
1 medium onion, peeled and chopped
3 green chillies, finely chopped
15 ml (1 tablespoon) mustard seeds
5 ml (1 teaspoon) coriander seeds
2 tomatoes, peeled and chopped

For serving
1 lemon, quartered

First make the filling. Cook the potatoes in boiling, salted water with the turmeric until they are just tender. Drain them and reserve 150 ml (¼ pint) of the water. Heat the oil in a pan and fry the onion over moderately high heat for 3–4 minutes, stirring once or twice. Stir in the chillies, mustard and coriander seeds and fry for 2 minutes. Add the potatoes, break them up with a wooden spoon and stir in the tomatoes and the reserved liquid. Simmer uncovered for 5 minutes, until most of the liquid has evaporated – the mixture should be moist but not wet. Keep the filling warm.

Put the batter ingredients into a blender and whizz. Oil an 18-cm (7-in) omelette pan and pour in just enough batter to cover the base thinly. Fry until the underside is brown. Flip or toss over and fry the other side. Slide the pancake on to a plate, cover and keep warm. Use the remaining batter to make 7 more pancakes in the same way.

Fill the pancakes with the potato mixture and fold them over. Serve hot.

Serves 4

* Sliced hard-boiled egg and a spiced pulse dish, such as Spiced chick-peas (page 200), are good accompaniments. So is Brinjal (aubergine) pickle.

SPINACH CRÊPES

50 g (2 oz) wholewheat flour
2.5 ml (½ teaspoon) salt
2 eggs
50 g (2 oz) butter, melted
150 ml (¼ pint) milk
75 ml (5 tablespoons) water
225 g (8 oz) frozen spinach, thawed and finely chopped
15 ml (1 tablespoon) chopped fresh sorrel or mint
oil, for frying

For the filling
450 g (1 lb) cottage cheese, sieved
60 ml (4 tablespoons) plain yoghurt
1 egg, beaten
salt and pepper
90 ml (6 tablespoons) Parmesan cheese, grated
2 carrots, cooked and finely diced
6 asparagus spears, cooked and chopped

Put the flour, salt, eggs, 30 ml (2 tablespoons) of the melted butter, the milk and water into a blender and whizz. Stir in the spinach and herb and add a little more water if necessary to make the batter the consistency of thin cream. Set aside for about 2 hours.

Oil and heat an 18-cm (7-in) omelette pan. Pour in 30–45 ml (2–3 tablespoons) of the mixture, tilt the pan so that it covers the base and cook over a moderately high heat until the crêpe bubbles. Toss or flip and cook the other side for a few moments. Stack the cooked crêpes on a plate over a pan of hot water and cover them with a cloth while you cook the remaining batter.

To make the filling, mix together the cottage cheese, yoghurt, beaten egg and 30 ml (2 tablespoons) of the parmesan cheese and season with salt and pepper. Stir in the vegetables.

Spoon a portion of the filling mixture into the centre of each crêpe and roll them loosely. Arrange them in a greased, shallow ovenproof dish and brush with the remaining butter. Sprinkle with the rest of the grated cheese and bake in a pre-heated oven, 180°C (350°F), Gas 4, for 20 minutes. *Serves 4–6*

MUSHROOM PIZZA

175 g (6 oz) 81 per cent self-raising flour
2.5 ml (½ teaspoon) baking powder
salt and pepper
50 g (2 oz) margarine
5 ml (1 teaspoon) mixed dried herbs
75 ml (5 tablespoons) plain yoghurt

For the filling
800-g (1 lb 12-oz) can tomatoes
2 cloves garlic, peeled and crushed
10 ml (2 teaspoons) dried basil
5 ml (1 teaspoon) dried thyme
15 ml (1 tablespoon) chopped fresh parsley
5 ml (1 teaspoon) light Muscovado sugar
salt and pepper
225 g (8 oz) button mushrooms, sliced
150 g (5 oz) Cheddar cheese, grated
1 green pepper, seeded and cut into rings
50 g (2 oz) black olives, halved and stoned

To make the filling, tip the tomatoes into a pan with the garlic, herbs and sugar, season with salt and pepper, bring to the boil and simmer for 10 minutes, until the sauce is thick. Set aside in a warm place.

Sift together the flour, baking powder, salt and pepper and rub in the margarine until the mixture is like crumbs. Stir in the herbs and yoghurt to form a soft dough. Knead until there are no cracks, then press into a 25-cm (10-in) greased flan ring placed on a greased baking sheet. Bake in a pre-heated oven, 200°C (400°F), Gas 6, for 15 minutes.

Spread the tomato sauce over the pizza, arrange the mushrooms, cover with the cheese and arrange the pepper rings and olives. Return to the oven for 10 minutes, or cook under a very hot grill. Serve hot.

Serves 2–3

* You can use 225 g (8 oz) wholewheat bread dough (page 234) in place of this scone-dough recipe.

8 Vegetable Accompaniments

How can you accompany vegetable dishes *with* vegetables, and not be boring? 'If I knew that,' a reader wrote recently, 'I'd become a vegetarian like a shot!' This chapter is for her!

Vegetables have all the virtues. Many of them – pulses, legumes, spinach and roots especially – are high in dietary fibre. And they are all so *individual*, full of their own flavour, colour and texture, that the permutations are baffling. With vegetable curry, perhaps you'd like spiced mung beans – the kind of dish we tend to refer to generically as dhal; with high-rise spinach soufflé, maybe a stir-fried selection including mushrooms and nuts; with aubergines packed with rice and dried fruits, I think I'd like steamed broccoli, and to accompany a vegetable quiche, I might choose runner beans *à la grecque*, both served slightly warm.

To be fair to fresh vegetables, you must cook them lightly, so that they retain the maximum possible nutrient content, colour and texture. Overcooked, they definitely lose their personalities and become less appetizing. Whether you steam them briskly over boiling water or stock; stir-fry them in a very little very hot oil, Chinese-style; simmer them in butter and just enough stock to provide steam for cooking, and then evaporate away; or cook them in boiling, salted water or stock, you *must* rescue them when they still slightly resist the point of a knife.

For a main serving, fresh vegetables should be cooked

moments before the meal; waiting around in the kitchen they lose nutrients. But small quantities of cooked or partly-cooked vegetables such as carrots and cauliflower florets are so useful in made-up dishes – risotto, stuffed vegetables, flans – that it's well worth cooking extra and storing them in a covered container in the refrigerator.

The same applies – only more so – to pulses of all kinds. With their much longer cooking times, it's good sense to cook extra to use in salads, stuffings, casseroles or as a garnish to fresh vegetables.

Wash all pulses in a bowl of cold water, discard any discoloured ones, those that float to the top, and bits of grit, then drain them. Lentils, split peas and mung beans may be cooked without soaking, though pre-soaking (re-hydrating) does cut down on cooking time.

Other pulses can be soaked for 3 or 4 hours or overnight, and will absorb roughly two-and-a-half times their dried volume. You can speed up the process by bringing them to the boil in unsalted water, boiling for 2 minutes, then leaving them in the pan to cool. Drain, and they're ready to cook.

Cooking times vary considerably with the type of pulse and its 'shelf-life'; the longer it has sat in a packet or jar, the longer it will take to cook. Pressure-cooking at high pressure cuts the cooking time by about 70 per cent. Fast-boil all kidney beans for at least 10 minutes before turning the heat down to simmer. And never add salt to the water when cooking any pulses – add it as a condiment right at the end. Salt inhibits the absorption process, and the poor old bean has to fight to come right.

COOKING TIMES FOR PULSES

45 minutes–1 hour
red lentils, unsoaked
green or brown lentils,
    unsoaked
split peas, soaked
mung beans, unsoaked

1–1½ hours
adzuki beans
butter beans or lima beans
black-eyed beans
flageolets
white haricot beans

kidney or navy beans
pinto beans
split peas, unsoaked

1½–2 hours
borlotti beans
broad beans or fava beans

2–2½ hours
chick-peas
soya beans (may take even
    longer)

BEETROOTS WITH CARAWAY

450 g (1 lb) small beetroots
salt
2 bay leaves
150 ml (¼ pint) soured cream
10 ml (2 teaspoons) caraway seeds
pepper

Tear off the leaves from the beetroots and cut off the roots
but do not break the skins. Wash well. Cook the beetroots in
boiling, salted water with the bay leaves for 1–1½ hours
(depending on size and age), or until they are tender. Drain
them and when they are cool enough to handle, rub off the
skins.

Slice the beetroots and toss back into the pan with the
soured cream and caraway seeds. Season with salt and
pepper and just heat through.
Serves 4

* You can serve them in Béchamel sauce, too – the beetroots colour it shocking pink. Add 30 ml (2 tablespoons) chopped chives.

CELERIAC

Since it's so very high in dietary fibre, it's worth getting to know this less familiar vegetable better.

    about 450 g (1 lb) celeriac
    30 ml (2 tablespoons) lemon juice
    salt
    150 ml (¼ pint) soured cream
    15 ml (1 tablespoon) chopped chives
    pepper

Trim off the root fibres and thinly peel the celeriac. Drop it at once into boiling water to which you have added half the lemon juice, and salt. Boil for 20–25 minutes, or until just tender. Drain.

When it is cool enough to handle, cut the celeriac into thin matchstick strips. Return it to the pan with the soured cream, chives and remaining lemon juice. Season with salt and pepper and just heat through.
Serves 4

KOHLRABI

Its name means 'cabbage turnip', from which you deduce that the stem bulges at the base to resemble a turnip, and produces brassica-like leaves at the top. Right!

    750 g (1½ lb) kohlrabi
    25 g (1 oz) butter
    150 ml (¼ pint) vegetable stock (page 12)

a few stalks parsley
salt and pepper
90 ml (6 tablespoons) double cream
5 ml (1 teaspoon) grated orange rind

For garnish
30 ml (2 tablespoons) chopped fresh parsley

Strip off the stems and leaves. You can cook them or eat them raw, as spinach, finely chopping the stems.

To prepare the 'bulbs', scrub them, and peel only if they are large and tough. Chop into 2.5-cm (1-in) cubes and put in a pan with the butter, stock and parsley stalks. Season the stock with salt and pepper, bring to the boil and cook, uncovered, for about 20 minutes, or until the vegetable is tender and the stock has evaporated. Discard the parsley, stir in the cream and orange rind and season with salt and pepper. Garnish with the chopped parsley.
Serves 4

* You can also serve kohlrabi in a Béchamel sauce, or make it into a purée, perhaps mixed half-and-half with potato purée and sprinkled with sunflower seeds.

BAKED SWEDE WITH CHEESE TOPPING

1 kg (2¼ lb) swede, roughly chopped
salt
50 g (2 oz) butter
60 ml (4 tablespoons) double cream
1 medium onion, peeled and chopped
4 stalks celery, thinly sliced
pepper
a large pinch of grated nutmeg

For the topping
60 ml (4 tablespoons) rolled porage oats
50 g (2 oz) Cheddar cheese, grated

Cook the swede in boiling, salted water for 20 minutes, until it is tender. Drain and mash it with half the butter and the cream.

Melt the remaining butter in a pan and fry the onion and celery over moderate heat, stirring once or twice, for 3 minutes. Beat these vegetables into the swede and season well with salt, pepper and nutmeg.

Turn the vegetable mixture into a well-greased casserole, mix together the oats and cheese and sprinkle over the top. Bake in a pre-heated oven, 190°C (375°F), Gas 5, for 25 minutes. Serve hot.
Serves 4–6

* Other root vegetables take well to cooking in this way – parsnips sparked up with the grated rind and juice of an orange; turnips with lemon; kohlrabi with 30 ml (2 tablespoons) chopped chervil or parsley; celeriac with chopped chives.

BAKED ORANGE POTATOES

A crispy side dish to make when you are using the oven to bake other vegetables.

750 g (1½ lb) potatoes, scrubbed
salt
40 g (1½ oz) butter
2 medium onions, peeled and sliced
grated rind and juice of 2 oranges
pepper

For garnish
watercress sprigs

Blanch the potatoes in boiling, salted water for 3 minutes. Drain and cut them into 2.5-cm (1-in) cubes and pat them dry. Melt the butter in a shallow flameproof dish and fry the onion over moderate heat for 3 minutes, stirring once or twice. Add the potatoes and cook for about 5 minutes, stirring often, until they are beginning to brown. Stir in the orange rind and juice and season with salt and pepper.

Cook, uncovered, in a pre-heated oven, 190°C (375°F), Gas 5, for about 35 minutes, stirring occasionally so that the potatoes brown evenly. Garnish with the watercress and serve hot.

Serves 4

POTATO SESAMES

750 g (1½ lb) potatoes, scrubbed
salt
45 ml (3 tablespoons) wholewheat flour
1 egg
15 ml (1 tablespoon) milk
105 ml (7 tablespoons) sesame seeds
oil, for frying

Cook the potatoes in boiling, salted water for about 10–12 minutes, until they are just beginning to soften. On no account overcook them. Drain and cut the potatoes into 12-mm (½-in) slices.

Toss the potato slices in the flour to coat them thoroughly. Mix together the egg and milk and dip the slices first in that, then in the sesame seeds so that they are well coated on both sides.

Heat the oil in a frying-pan and fry the potato slices in a single layer over moderate heat for 3 minutes, until they are

well browned. Turn the slices and cook for 2-3 minutes on the other side. Serve at once.
Serves 4

* As an alternative, toss the potato slices just in rolled porage oats (no need for a flour and egg foundation); they're delicious that way too.

BROAD BEANS WITH CELERY

1 kg (2¼ lb) fresh broad beans
40 g (1½ oz) butter
1 medium onion, peeled and sliced
4 stalks celery, thinly sliced
150 ml (¼ pint) vegetable stock (page 12)
30 ml (2 tablespoons) chopped fresh summer savory, or
   mint
salt and pepper
60 ml (4 tablespoons) cooked flageolets
60 ml (4 tablespoons) double cream

Shell the broad beans. Melt the butter in a pan and fry the onion and celery over moderate heat for about 3 minutes, stirring once or twice. Add the broad beans, stock and herb, salt and pepper, bring to the boil, cover and simmer for 15 minutes, or until the beans are just tender. Stir in the flageolets and cream and add more seasoning if necessary. Just heat through, and serve hot.
Serves 4

RUNNER BEANS À LA GRECQUE

Prepare it up to two days ahead and serve as a first course or side-dish. It's especially good with all egg dishes.

1 small onion, peeled and thinly sliced
2 cloves garlic, peeled and crushed

2 stalks celery, thinly sliced
60 ml (4 tablespoons) olive oil
60 ml (4 tablespoons) cider vinegar
30 ml (2 tablespoons) tomato purée
350 ml (12 fl oz) water
5 ml (1 teaspoon) dried savory
1 bouquet garni
2 bay leaves
8 black peppercorns, lightly crushed
8 coriander seeds, lightly crushed
2.5 ml (½ teaspoon) salt
650 g (1¼ lb) young runner beans, topped, tailed, strings
removed

For garnish
30 ml (2 tablespoons) chopped fresh parsley

Put the first thirteen ingredients into a pan, bring to the boil, cover the pan and simmer for 30 minutes. Slice the beans diagonally into 2.5-cm (1-in) lengths and add to the pan. Bring back to the boil and simmer for 7–8 minutes, or until the beans are just tender. Remove them, fast-boil the sauce for 5 minutes, taste and adjust the seasoning if needed. Strain the sauce on to the beans.

Sprinkle with the parsley just before serving. Serve hot (which is somewhat unconventional) or cold – in which case the dish can be stored in a covered container in the refrigerator for up to two days.

Serves 4

* There's masses of scope for other high-fibre vegetables to be cooked in a similar way. French beans, strips of carrots, cauliflower florets, young celery hearts, whole or sliced mushrooms are all traditional. Vary the herbs and spices, substitute some red or white wine for the water and make each experiment excitingly different from the last.

SPRING VEGETABLE MEDLEY

Green beans are tops for fibre. Here's a way to add colour and interest.

450 g (1 lb) young French beans, topped and tailed
salt
25 g (1 oz) butter
16 very small onions, or shallots, peeled
4 medium carrots, thickly sliced
120 ml (8 tablespoons) vegetable stock (page 12)
15 ml (1 tablespoon) light Muscovado sugar
60 ml (4 tablespoons) cooked haricot beans
60 ml (4 tablespoons) double cream
pepper

For garnish
30 ml (2 tablespoons) chopped fresh parsley

Cut the beans diagonally into 5-cm (2-in) pieces and blanch them in boiling, salted water for 3 minutes, then drain.

Melt the butter in a pan and fry the whole onions over moderate heat, stirring often, for 4 minutes. Stir in the carrots to glaze them, then pour on the stock. Add the sugar, cover and simmer for 10 minutes. Add the French beans and the haricots and simmer uncovered for 2–3 minutes until the stock has been absorbed. Stir in the cream and season the vegetables with salt and pepper. Serve hot, garnished with the parsley.

Serves 4

STIR-FRIED MANGE-TOUT PEAS

It's a very short season that we can enjoy these 'eatpod and all' young peas – this is a delightful way to savour them.

450 g (1 lb) mange-tout peas, topped, tailed, strings removed
salt
30 ml (2 tablespoons) dry sherry
15 ml (1 tablespoon) soy sauce
10 ml (2 teaspoons) light Muscovado sugar
45 ml (3 tablespoons) water
60 ml (4 tablespoons) oil
2 spring onions, peeled and thinly sliced
2 cloves garlic, peeled and crushed
1 green pepper, trimmed, seeded and thinly sliced
100 g (4 oz) button mushrooms, sliced
50 g (2 oz) blanched almonds, split

Have all the ingredients ready prepared. Slice the pea pods into 3 pieces if they are large. Very young and small ones – by far the tastiest – can be left whole. Blanch them in boiling, salted water for 3 minutes, then drain. Mix together the sherry, sauce, sugar and water.

Heat the oil in a pan and stir-fry the onion and garlic over moderately high heat for 1 minute. Toss in the pepper and mushrooms and stir-fry for 2 minutes; add the almonds and cook for 1 minute, then stir in the sauce. Bring to the boil and fast-boil for 2 minutes. Toss in the peas, stir well, lower the heat and simmer for 1 minute. (Sorry, but it takes longer to describe than to cook!) Season with salt and serve at once.
Serves 4

GREEN AND CREAM

Peas and sweetcorn, perfect colour partners, and vying with each other for fibre content!

1 kg (2¼ lb) fresh peas
12–16 very small onions or shallots, peeled
350 g (12 oz) frozen sweetcorn, thawed
90 ml (6 tablespoons) vegetable stock (page 12)
40 g (1½ oz) butter
salt and pepper
30 ml (2 tablespoons) chopped fresh mint
60 ml (4 tablespoons) double cream

Shell the peas. Blanch the onions in boiling water for 30 minutes, then drain. Put the onions, peas and sweetcorn in a pan with the stock and butter, bring to the boil, cover and simmer for 10–12 minutes, or until the vegetables are tender and the stock has been absorbed. Season with salt and pepper and stir in the mint and the cream. Serve at once. *Serves 4*

BRUSSELS SPROUTS WITH CHESTNUTS

Traditionally served at Christmas-time – but why only then?

450 g (1 lb) chestnuts
40 g (1½ oz) butter
300 ml (½ pint) vegetable stock (page 12)
a few parsley stalks
2 bay leaves
750 g (1½ lb) Brussels sprouts, trimmed
salt and pepper

Prick the chestnut skins, place the nuts in a pan of cold water, bring to the boil then remove from the heat. Peel off the skins.

Melt half the butter in a pan, stir in the nuts to coat them, add the stock, parsley stalks and bay leaves and bring to the boil. Cover the pan and simmer for 1 hour or until the nuts are tender. Discard the herbs and boil away any stock that has not been absorbed.

Steam the Brussels sprouts over salted water for 10–12 minutes, or until they are just tender. Add the remaining butter to the now-dry pan of chestnuts, stir in the cooked sprouts and season with salt and pepper. Serve at once.
Serves 4

* Very lightly-cooked white cabbage is especially good with chestnuts, too. They really give it a face-lift!

SPINACH AND COURGETTE TOSS

    450 g (1 lb) courgettes, grated
    salt
    450 g (1 lb) spinach
    25 g (1 oz) butter
    15 ml (1 tablespoon) oil
    50 g (2 oz) blanched almonds, split
    1 medium onion, peeled and chopped
    1 clove garlic, peeled and crushed
    pepper

Put the courgettes into a colander and sprinkle with salt. Leave to drain for 30 minutes, then rinse, drain again and pat dry. Strip the spinach leaves from the stalks and blanch the leaves in boiling, salted water for 2 minutes. Drain thoroughly and chop.

Heat the butter and oil in a pan and fry the almonds until they are brown. Remove them and set aside. Add the onions and garlic to the pan and fry over moderate heat for 3 minutes, stirring once or twice. Add the courgettes, stir well and cook for 2 minutes. Stir in the spinach, mixing well, and simmer for 5 minutes, or until the vegetables are just tender. Season liberally with salt and pepper and stir in the almonds. Serve at once.

Serves 4

STIR-FRIED SPRING GREENS

They don't have a very glamorous image, do they? But this way, crisply tender and retaining all their rich colour, they might surprise you.

1 kg (2¼ lb) young spring greens
25 g (1 oz) butter
30 ml (2 tablespoons) oil
salt
10 ml (2 teaspoons) lemon juice
30 ml (2 tablespoons) sweet sherry
pepper
a pinch of grated nutmeg
45 ml (3 tablespoons) cashew nuts

Strip away the tough stems and thoroughly wash and drain the greens, then cut them into 2.5-cm (1-in) strips. Melt the butter and oil in a heavy-based frying-pan and when it is hot, add the greens and stir-fry them over moderately high heat for 2 minutes. Add the salt, lemon juice and sherry, stir well and lower the heat to moderate. Cover the pan and simmer for 5 minutes, stirring once or twice. Season with pepper and nutmeg and test with a sharp knife point or skewer. Cook for a further 2–3 minutes if necessary – this will depend on the age of the vegetables. They should be only just tender. Scatter the greens with the cashews and serve at once – they lose crispness if they have to wait around.

Serves 4

* Cook broccoli spears in the same way, cut diagonally into 4-cm (1½-in) slices.

VEGETABLE FRITTERS

Puffed-up and crisply golden, fritters offer an exciting contrast in texture to practically every main dish you can mention. Make them of a single vegetable – celery or mushrooms, say – or a selection, when they can be an exciting meal in themselves (page 170).

2 heads young celery
salt
45 ml (3 tablespoons) oil
15 ml (1 tablespoon) lemon juice
pepper
oil, for deep frying

For the batter
150 g (5 oz) wholewheat flour
15 ml (1 tablespoon) bran
salt
15 ml (1 tablespoon) oil
1 egg, separated
200 ml (7 fl oz) milk (or you can use beer)

For serving
1 lemon, quartered

Use only the white and tender base of the stalks to cook in this way. Reserve the green and tougher parts for soup or casseroles.

Cut the celery into 2.5-cm (1-in) strips and blanch them in boiling, salted water for 4 minutes. Drain and pat them dry. Whisk together the oil and lemon juice, season with salt and pepper and marinate the celery for 1 hour. Drain and pat dry again.

To make the batter, mix together the flour, bran and salt and beat in the oil and egg yolk. Gradually beat in the milk or beer (or use an electric blender or food processor for speed and smoothness). Cover the bowl and leave to stand for 1 hour. Stiffly beat the egg white and fold it in just before using.

In a pan, heat the oil to a temperature of 190°C (375°F). (At this heat a cube of day-old bread browns in 50 seconds.) Dip the celery in the batter and fry in batches for 4–5 minutes, or until golden and crisp. Toss on kitchen paper to dry and serve at once, garnished with the lemon wedges.
Serves 4

BAKED MUSHROOMS AND TOMATOES

8 large mushrooms
1 small onion, peeled and finely chopped
15 g (1½ oz) margarine
90 ml (6 tablespoons) wholewheat breadcrumbs
40 g (½ oz) Cheddar cheese, grated
50 g (2 oz) canned sweetcorn, drained
5 ml (1 teaspoon) chopped fresh mint
2.5 ml (½ teaspoon) dried oregano
salt and pepper
1 egg, beaten
2 large tomatoes, halved

For garnish
4 slices wholewheat bread, toasted

Chop the mushroom stalks and mix with the onion. Melt the margarine in a pan and fry the mushroom stalks and onion over moderate heat for about 3 minutes. Remove from the heat and stir in the breadcrumbs, cheese, sweetcorn and herbs, season with salt and pepper and bind with the egg.

Arrange the mushrooms, undersides up, and the tomatoes, cut sides up, in a greased shallow baking dish. Spoon the cheese mixture into the mushroom caps and on to the

H.F.V.C.-I

tomatoes, pressing it well down. Cover with foil and bake for 20 minutes in a pre-heated oven 190°C (375°F), Gas 5.

Garnish the dish with small triangles of toast.

Serves 4

RED CABBAGE WITH SULTANAS

1 medium red cabbage
25 g (1 oz) margarine
2 medium onions, peeled and sliced
150 ml (¼ pint) water
60 ml (4 tablespoons) red wine vinegar
30 ml (2 tablespoons) dark Muscovado sugar
5 ml (1 teaspoon) salt
15 ml (1 tablespoon) redcurrant jelly
60 ml (4 tablespoons) sultanas

For garnish
2 dessert apples, cored and thinly sliced
15 ml (1 tablespoon) lemon juice

Cut away the thick stalk and shred the cabbage finely. Melt the margarine in a pan and stir in the cabbage and onion. Pour on the water and vinegar and stir in the sugar and salt. Bring to the boil, cover and simmer gently for 2 hours, or until the cabbage is tender. Stir in the jelly and sultanas.

Toss the apple slices in lemon juice and arrange on the cabbage to garnish. Serve hot.

Serves 6–8

* Use raisins or chopped prunes instead of sultanas as an alternative.

VEGETABLE CROQUETTES

It's a question of mashed-potato-plus – plus whatever flavouring vegetables you have to hand. Chopped carrots, mushrooms or celery would be good, too.

350 g (12 oz) potatoes, scrubbed
3 small leeks, well washed and trimmed
salt
25 g (1 oz) margarine
2 eggs, lightly beaten
75 g (3 oz) ground hazelnuts
15 ml (1 tablespoon) chopped fresh parsley
pepper
30 ml (2 tablespoons) wholewheat flour
50 g (2 oz) wholewheat breadcrumbs
oil, for deep or shallow frying

For garnish
1 lemon, quartered

Cook the potatoes and leeks separately in boiling, salted water until they are tender, then drain them thoroughly. Chop the vegetables roughly and liquidize them in a blender. Beat in the margarine, half the beaten egg, 50 g (2 oz) of the nuts, the parsley, and season well with salt and pepper. Leave the mixture to cool.

Shape the paste into 12 'sausages' and roll them first in flour, then in the remaining egg, then in the crumbs mixed with the remaining nuts.

Heat the oil and fry the croquettes until they are evenly golden brown. Serve hot, garnished with the lemon wedges.
Serves 4

REAL BAKED BEANS

450 g (1 lb) dried haricot beans, soaked overnight and
   drained
2 medium onions, peeled and sliced
2 cloves garlic, peeled and crushed
4 stalks celery, thinly sliced
2 tomatoes, peeled and sliced
1 bouquet garni
15 ml (1 tablespoon) molasses
1.1 litres (2 pints) vegetable stock (page 12), boiling
salt and pepper

For garnish
30 ml (2 tablespoons) chopped fresh parsley

Put the beans in a casserole with the other vegetables, herbs
and molasses, pour on the stock and stir well. Cook in a pre-
heated oven, 150°C (300°F), Gas 2, for 2–2¼ hours, or until
the beans are just tender. Top up with more boiling stock if
necessary. Discard the herbs, season with salt and pepper
and garnish with the chopped parsley. Serve hot.
Serves 6–8

* For extra flavour toss 100 g (4 oz) sliced button
mushroms to cook in 25 g (1 oz) herb- or garlic-butter
(page 264) and stir them into the beans 10 minutes before the
end of cooking time.

BEAN AND APRICOT CASSEROLE

175 g (6 oz) dried white haricot beans, soaked overnight
   and drained
100 g (4 oz) dried apricots, soaked
40 g (1½ oz) butter
salt and pepper

For garnish
15 ml (1 tablespoon) chopped fresh parsley

Cook the beans in plenty of unsalted water for 1 hour, or until they are tender. Cook the apricots in the water in which they were soaked, for about 20 minutes or until they are just tender. Do not let them break up. Drain the beans and the apricots, toss them together in a pan with the butter and season with salt and pepper. Garnish with the parsley. Serve hot.

A good accompaniment to baked courgettes or tomatoes. *Serves 4*

KIDNEY BEAN CHILLI

225 g (8 oz) dried red kidney beans, soaked overnight and drained
45 ml (3 tablespoons) oil
2 medium onions, peeled and thinly sliced
2 cloves garlic, peeled and finely chopped
5 ml (1 teaspoon) paprika
2.5–5 ml (½–1 teaspoon) cayenne pepper
2.5 ml (½ teaspoon) ground allspice
30 ml (2 tablespoons) tomato purée
600 ml (1 pint) vegetable stock (page 12)
2 bay leaves
1 bouquet garni
15 ml (1 tablespoon) dark Muscovado sugar
15 ml (1 tablespoon) red wine vinegar
salt

For garnish
25 g (1 oz) butter
2 dessert apples, cored and thinly sliced

Boil the beans in unsalted water for 15 minutes, then drain. Heat the oil in a flameproof casserole and fry the onion and garlic for about 3 minutes, stirring once or twice. Stir in the spices and cook for 1 minute. Stir the tomato purée into the stock and add to the casserole with the herbs, beans, sugar and vinegar. Bring to the boil, cover and cook in a pre-heated oven, 180°C (350°F), Gas 4, for about 1¾ hours, or until the beans are tender. Discard the herbs, taste and adjust the seasoning if necessary.

For the garnish, melt the butter and fry the apple slices over moderate heat for about 2 minutes on each side until they are light brown. Arrange them on top of the beans and serve hot.

Serves 4

PEA PURÉE JAFFA

An occasion when it pays to plan ahead – you need a few cooked carrots!

225 g (8 oz) split yellow peas, washed and drained
60 ml (4 tablespoons) oil
2 medium onions, peeled and chopped
3 stalks celery, thinly sliced
2.5 ml (½ teaspoon) ground turmeric
2.5 ml (½ teaspoon) garam masala
5 ml (1 teaspoon) ground coriander
2 oranges
225 g (8 oz) cooked carrots, finely diced
salt and pepper

For garnish
2 spring onions, peeled and thinly sliced

Cook the split peas in boiling, unsalted water for 1-1½

hours, or until they are tender (this will depend on age). Drain and beat them to a purée.

Heat the oil in a pan and fry the onion and celery over moderate heat for 3 minutes, stirring once or twice. Stir in the spices and cook for 1 minute, then add the grated rind and juice of the oranges. Simmer for 2–3 minutes then stir in the pea purée and mix well. Lastly, stir in the carrots. Season with salt and pepper and heat through. Garnish with the sliced spring onions and serve hot.

Serves 4

PEASE PUDDING

Years ago it was made in a cloth, suspended inside a pot of simmering broth of roots and herbs. Serve it in thick, buttery slices with baked vegetables.

350 g (12 oz) dried split green peas, washed and drained
a bunch of parsley stalks
2 bay leaves
50 g (2 oz) butter
1 egg, beaten
5 ml (1 teaspoon) ground coriander
salt and pepper

For garnish
parsley sprigs

Cook the peas with the parsley stalks and bay leaves in plenty of boiling, unsalted water for 1–1½ hours, or until they are really tender (the time will depend on the age of the pulses). Drain the peas (discarding the herbs) and beat in the butter and egg. Season with the coriander, salt and pepper.

Turn the purée into a well-greased ovenproof bowl or basin and cover tightly with foil. Bake in a pre-heated oven, 180°C

(350°F), Gas 4, for 1 hour, or until the purée is set firm.
Garnish with the parsley and serve hot.
Serves 4–6

SPICED CHICK-PEAS

You can serve this dish as a 'starter', with Feta cheese and
raw onion rings, or as a side-dish, especially good with egg or
vegetable curries.

    225 g (8 oz) dried chick-peas, soaked overnight and
        drained
    60 ml (4 tablespoons) oil
    5 ml (1 teaspoon) cumin seeds
    1 medium onion, peeled and sliced
    2 cloves garlic, peeled and crushed
    10 ml (2 teaspoons) garam masala
    2.5 ml (½ teaspoon) cayenne pepper
    5 ml (1 teaspoon) ground ginger
    15 ml (1 tablespoon) lemon juice
    30 ml (2 tablespoons) tomato purée
    100 ml (3½ fl oz) water
    salt

    For garnish
    parsley sprigs

Cook the chick-peas in plenty of boiling, unsalted water for
about 2½ hours, or until they are tender.

Heat the oil in a pan and fry the cumin seeds over
moderate heat, stirring, for 1 minute, until they burst. Add
the onion and garlic and fry, stirring once or twice, for 3
minutes, then stir in the ground spices. After 1 minute, add
the lemon juice, tomato purée and water, stir well then add
the cooked peas. Simmer for 10 minutes, until the sauce

thickly coats the pulses. Season with salt and garnish with the parsley sprigs. Serve hot.
Serves 4

* Cook other pulses in a similar way – kidney beans of all shapes and sizes take well to this treatment.

SPROUTING CHICK-PEAS

When you've watched them grow in a lidded jar, it's fun to try new ways to serve sprouting beans and peas.

15 ml (1 tablespoon) oil
3 medium onions, peeled and sliced
2 cloves garlic, peeled and crushed
425-g (15-oz) can tomatoes
5 ml (1 teaspoon) dried oregano
salt and pepper
175 g (6 oz) sprouting chick-peas (or other sprouting seeds), washed and drained
30 ml (2 tablespoons) chopped fresh mint
30 ml (2 tablespoons) Parmesan cheese grated

Heat the oil in a pan, fry the onions and garlic over moderate heat for 3 minutes, stirring once or twice, add the tomatoes and oregano and season with salt and pepper. Bring to the boil and simmer briskly for 15 minutes, until the sauce thickens. Add the sprouting peas, stir and simmer for 5 minutes. Stir in the mint, sprinkle with the cheese and serve hot.
Serves 4

SPICED MUNG BEANS

An appetizingly green side-dish, an alternative to lentil dhal.

350 g (12 oz) dried mung beans, washed and drained
45 g (3 tablespoons) oil
2 medium onions, peeled and sliced
2 cloves garlic, peeled and crushed
5 ml (1 teaspoon) ground coriander
5 ml (1 teaspoon) cumin seeds
5 ml (1 teaspoon) garam masala
2 tomatoes
15 ml (1 tablespoon) lemon juice
salt

For garnish
1 lemon, quartered
1 tomato, quartered

Cook the beans in plenty of unsalted water for about 1 hour, or until they are just tender. Drain.

Heat the oil in a pan and fry the onion and garlic over moderate heat for 3 minutes, stirring once or twice. Add the spices and stir for 1 minute. Peel and chop the tomatoes and stir them into the mixture with the lemon juice and salt.

Add the cooked beans to the pan and simmer very gently for 5 minutes, stirring to prevent from sticking.

Garnish the dish with lemon and tomato wedges. Serve hot.

Serves 4–6

9 Fruit Salads

Whilst all fresh fruit salads are packed with vitamins, they are not all as bursting with fibre as one might think. But there are ways! Of the fresh fruits, black, red and white currants, blackberries, loganberries and raspberries come out top. So in mixed fruit salads, it's a good idea to use these fruits (rather than grapes, cherries or strawberries, for example) for the bright colour or small compact shapes that are needed.

Another trick is to make a sauce using whole berry fruits and toss sliced orchard fruits into it. Raspberry sauce poured over fresh peaches, pears or strawberries – even better if it's tossed on to more fresh raspberries – is out of this world. Blackberry sauce with wafer-thin slices of apple or quartered pears is quite an experience. And so easy!

Adding blanched or toasted nuts, a handful of raisins or sultanas, all provides more texture and colour variation – and that valuable fibre.

But which fruits are already brimming over with it? The answer is all the dried fruits you care to mention. Dried apricots, for example, contain 24 per cent dietary fibre, fresh apricots only 2.1 per cent; dried peaches have 14.3 per cent, fresh ones only 1.4 per cent. Even without a calculator, I figure that's an advantage factor of more than ten times.

So, not surprisingly, you will come across a few ideas in the following pages to maximize on this. Dried fruit salads of cooked or macerated apples, apricots, peaches, pears, prunes, dates, figs, sultanas and nuts are very much a feature of Middle Eastern cooking, often delicately flavoured with a hint of rosewater or orangeflower water. And so I've taken a leaf out of their book, though in the decadent West we sometimes stir in a drop of brandy, too! These salads are equally good hot or chilled and to my mind are better served with plain yoghurt or soured cream than with whipped or double cream.

A salad combining fresh and dried fruits of the same or different types gives a delicious balance of melt-in-the-mouth and crisp, crunchy textures – try dried and fresh pears or apricots together and you will want to experiment with other partnerships.

Yet another way is to make a golden, dreamy sauce of dried apricots, or other fruits, lightly spiced if you wish, to toss over dried apple rings, fresh apple slices, melon balls – you name it. It may be cheating, but it's a fabulous way to take fibre!

AVOCADO CUPS

    2 large, ripe avocados
    30 ml (2 tablespoons) lemon juice
    2 dessert apples, cored and thinly sliced
    225 g (8 oz) blackberries, hulled
    100 g (4 oz) prunes, stoned and halved
    15 ml (1 tablespoon) clear honey
    150 ml (¼ pint) soured cream

    For decoration
    4 sprigs mint

Halve the avocados, remove the stones and scoop the flesh from the skins. Cut it into cubes and toss at once into the lemon juice. Add the apple slices and toss to coat them thoroughly. Pour off and reserve the remaining lemon juice.

Mix the blackberries and prunes with the other fruit. Stir the honey into the remaining lemon juice, then beat in the soured cream. Pour the dressing over the fruit, mix well and pile into the avocado shells. Decorate with the mint sprigs. Serve chilled.

Serves 4

EVERYDAY FRUIT SALAD

Vary the fruits according to seasonal availability and you could serve a different permutation practically every day. In this mixture, the berries, sultanas and nuts provide the high fibre.

    2 dessert apples, cored and thinly sliced
    2 pears, cored and sliced
    450 g (1 lb) raspberries, loganberries or blackberries,
       hulled
    50 g (2 oz) sultanas
    3 bananas, sliced
    50 g (2 oz) blanched almonds, split

    For the syrup
    225 ml (8 fl oz) unsweetened apple juice
    juice of 1 lemon
    1 strip of lemon peel
    1 stick cinnamon

To make the sauce, bring the apple juice and lemon juice to the boil with the lemon peel and cinnamon. Leave to cool and discard the flavourings.

Toss the apples, pears, raspberries and sultanas into the syrup and chill. Just before serving, stir in the bananas and almonds.

Serves 6

DOMINO SALAD

450 g (1 lb) dessert blackberries, hulled
150 ml (¼ pint) black grape juice
3 bananas, sliced
2 dessert apples, cored and thinly sliced

For serving
225 g (8 oz) cottage cheese, chilled
40 g (1½ oz) desiccated coconut

Mix together the blackberries, grape juice, bananas and apples. Stir the cottage cheese and coconut together and form into walnut-sized balls. Just before serving, scatter the cheese balls over the salad.
Serves 4

BLACKCURRANT AND APPLE COMPOTE

450 g (1 lb) blackcurrants, stripped from stalks
45 ml (3 tablespoons) water
50 g (2 oz) light Muscovado sugar
2 dessert apples, cored and thinly sliced

Stir the water and sugar in a pan over low heat until the sugar dissolves. Bring to the boil, add the blackcurrants and bring slowly back to the boil – do not let the fruit 'collapse'. Pour the hot fruit over the sliced apples, cool and then chill.
Serves 4

RASPBERRY SAUCE WITH PEACHES

We call this 'ubiquitous' sauce at home, because it goes so perfectly with fruit of all kinds. It's a way of adding fibre to the low-count but delicious summer fruits – peaches, pears, cherries, strawberries.

6 large, ripe peaches, stoned and thinly sliced

For the sauce
750 g (1½ lb) raspberries, hulled
30 ml (2 tablespoons) water
juice and thinly-pared rind of 1 lemon
100 g (4 oz) icing sugar

For serving
50 g (2 oz) blanched almonds, toasted

To make the sauce, put the raspberries in a pan with the water, lemon juice and rind and cook over very low heat until the juice begins to run. Bring slowly to the boil and carefully stir in the sugar without breaking up the fruit. As soon as it has dissolved remove the pan from the heat.

Pour the hot sauce over the peaches and leave to cool. Chill; scatter over the almonds before serving.
Serves 6

* Make a similar sauce with blackberries, loganberries, red- or blackcurrants. They're all high in fibre and fabulous with orchard fruits.

REDCURRANT COCKTAIL

750 g (1½ lb) redcurrants, stripped from stalks
3 oranges
75 ml (3 tablespoons) honey

For serving
30 ml (2 tablespoons) pine nuts

Squeeze the juice from all the oranges and grate the rind from one. Put juice and rind in a pan with the honey and stir just until the honey melts. Pour over the redcurrants, cool then chill. Scatter with the nuts to serve.
Serves 4

MELON AND BANANA IN RAISIN SAUCE

1 medium honeydew melon
3 slightly under-ripe bananas, thinly sliced

For the sauce
45 ml (3 tablespoons) honey
75 ml (5 tablespoons) water
15 ml (1 tablespoon) lemon juice
a strip lemon peel
15 ml (1 tablespoon) rum
100 g (4 oz) seedless raisins

Begin by making the sauce. Put all the ingredients in a pan, bring to the boil and simmer for 5 minutes. Cool, then chill.

Using a vegetable baller or teaspoon, scoop out spheres of the melon flesh. Mix them with the banana slices, pour on the sauce and serve at once.
Serves 4

MACERATED ORANGES

By themselves, oranges don't rate very highly in the fibre charts, but tossed with apricots and nuts they do. A perfect winter salad.

6 large oranges
225 g (8 oz) dried apricots, soaked and drained
225 g (8 fl oz) sweet white wine
15 ml (1 tablespoon) orangeflower water
100 g (4 oz) blanched almonds, split

Peel and very thinly slice 4 of the oranges – an electric carving knife does the job to perfection. Arrange the orange slices in a bowl with the apricots. Squeeze the juice from the other 2 oranges and mix it with the wine and orangeflower

water and pour over the fruit. Leave to macerate for at least 3 hours. Scatter with the almonds. Serve chilled.
Serves 4

STRAIGHT-FROM-THE-JAR SALAD

Well, after macerating for two days, that is! A delicious way to serve dried fruits.

  100 g (4 oz) dried apricots
  100 g (4 oz) prunes, stoned
  100 g (4 oz) dried figs
  60 ml (4 tablespoons) sultanas
  15 ml (1 tablespoon) rosewater
  30 ml (2 tablespoons) walnut halves
  30 ml (2 tablespoons) brazil nuts
  30 ml (2 tablespoons) brandy (optional)

Put the dried fruits in a bowl and cover them with water; add the rosewater and cover with a lid. Macerate in the refrigerator for two days. Before serving, stir in the nuts and the brandy if using. Delicious with soured cream.
Serves 6

ARABIAN DELIGHT

  450 g (1 lb) mixed dried orchard fruits, e.g. apricots, peaches, pears, prunes
  100 g (4 oz) sultanas
  1 stick cinnamon
  1 strip lemon peel
  30 ml (2 tablespoons) rosewater, or orangeflower water
  75 g (3 oz) blanched almonds, split

Soak the orchard fruits in water for 3–4 hours or overnight. Measure 850 ml (1½ pints) of the soaking water into a pan. Add the soaked fruit, the sultanas, cinnamon and lemon peel, bring to the boil and simmer for 30 minutes. Discard the cinnamon and lemon peel and stir in the flower water and almonds. Serve hot or cold.

Serves 4

GOLDEN RINGS

Apricot purée makes a glowing golden sauce that enhances fruits of all kinds. Try it with sliced fresh apples, melon cubes or steamed rhubarb.

    225 g (8 oz) dried apricots, soaked
    1 stick cinnamon
    225 g (8 oz) dried apple rings, soaked and drained
    225 g (8 oz) fresh dates, stoned
    60 ml (4 tablespoons) blanched almonds, toasted

Cook the apricots in the soaking water with the cinnamon for about 30 minutes. Drain them and reserve the liquid. Liquidize the fruit in a blender with 125 ml (4 fl oz) of the cooking liquid. Cook the apple rings in the remaining apricot liquid for 5 minutes, or until they are just tender – do not let them 'collapse'.

Lift out the apple rings with a draining spoon, arrange them in a shallow serving dish and scatter with the dates. Pour over the apricot purée and decorate with the toasted almonds. Serve cold.

Serves 4

PEARS TIMES TWO

A good way to enjoy the best of both worlds is to combine fresh and dried fruits of the same type.

225 g (8 oz) dried pears, quartered, soaked and drained
450 ml (¾ pint) unsweetened orange juice
15 ml (1 tablespoon) lemon juice
1 stick cinnamon
100 g (4 oz) fresh dates, stoned
4 ripe dessert pears, peeled, cored and quartered

Put the dried pears, orange juice, lemon juice and cinnamon in a pan, bring slowly to the boil and simmer for 20 minutes. Add the dates and leave to cool. Discard the cinnamon, stir in the fresh pear slices and chill.
Serves 4

* Add a little honey to the orange juice if you wish; though the pears sweeten it quite considerably.

* Follow this formula with dried and fresh apricots.

10   Other Puddings

Good old nursery puds, though we probably didn't realize it at the time, were full of fibre. Baked bread and butter pudding with lots of currants; steamed fruit puds sticky with figs or dates; rice pudding; baked apples packed with nuts and raisins – they were all among the good guys. More sophisticated desserts too, the kind we turn to for dinner parties, can be just as rewarding, fibre-wise. Hazelnut meringue torte filled with berry fruits; home-made ice cream crunchy with praline; chestnut gâteau – they all have a good count.

Just using wholewheat flour in steamed and baked puddings; brown rice instead of its polished equivalent; wholewheat semolina for milk puddings and for thickening; adding a sprinkling of nuts or seeds at the slightest opportunity; choosing the highest-fibre fruits, or mixing them with others – if you follow these simple guidelines the pudding course can make a significant contribution.

PRALINE ICE CREAM

Fresh raspberries make a lovely accompaniment to this nutty ice cream.

300 ml (½ pint) single cream
4 egg yolks
300 ml (½ pint) double cream, whipped
75 g (3 oz) light Muscovado sugar

For the praline
175 g (6 oz) light Muscovado sugar
15 ml (1 tablespoon) water
175 g (6 oz) unblanched almonds

Boil the single cream then beat it into the egg yolks. Turn the mixture into a double boiler or a bowl fitted over a pan of simmering water and whisk until it thickens enough to coat the back of a spoon – about 10 minutes. Strain and cool. Fold in the whipped cream and 125 g (5 oz) of the crushed praline (see below).

Pour into a chilled container, cover with foil and freeze for 1 hour. Turn the mixture into a chilled bowl, beat it well, cover and freeze for a further 2 hours.

Leave the ice cream to rest in the main part of the refrigerator for at least 30 minutes before serving. Serve in scoops, sprinkled with more crushed praline.

To make the praline, put the sugar and water into a pan and stir over low heat to dissolve the sugar. Add the almonds and bring slowly to the boil. Increase the heat until the sugar caramelizes and turns golden brown. Stir to toast the nuts evenly. Turn the mixture into a well-greased Swiss roll tin and leave to cool. Crush by breaking the praline in pieces and whizzing in a blender, or roll vigorously between greaseproof paper with a rolling pin.

Store the crushed praline in a lidded jar.
Serves 6

* The praline has all kinds of uses – stir it into whipped cream to fill meringues; sprinkle it on fruit fool or fruit-flavoured ice cream; or stir it into sweet crumble toppings.

RASPBERRY FOOL

750 g (1½ lb) raspberries, hulled
40 g (1½ oz) light Muscovado sugar

300 ml (½ pint) double cream, stiffly whipped
30 ml (2 tablespoons) sweet sherry
45 ml (3 tablespoons) rolled porage oats, toasted (see below)

Reserve about 45 ml (3 tablespoons) of the best raspberries for decoration. Purée the remainder with the sugar in a blender. Turn the purée into a bowl and fold in first the cream, then the sherry.

Spoon the fruit mixture into a serving dish or individual glasses, sprinkle with the toasted oats and decorate with the whole fruit. Serve chilled, with Wholefood shortbread biscuits (page 252).
Serves 4

* It's a good idea to keep a supply of toasted oats in a lidded jar – they're useful for last-minute decorations, especially with creamy puds. Spread the oats on a baking tray and bake in the oven at 180°C (350°F), Gas 4, for 15 minutes, stirring them once or twice. Cool before storing.

* Use other fruits too for this quick and easy, but very tasty, dessert. Simmer gooseberries gently without water for 10 minutes, then liquidize, cool and fold in the cream. A head of elderflower (in the hedgerows when gooseberries are in the gardens) steeped in the fruit as it cooks makes a world of difference.

YOGHURT AMBROSIA

A candidate for the label of 'easiest sweet around'.

150 ml (¼ pint) plain yoghurt
150 ml (¼ pint) double cream
50 g (2 oz) crushed praline (page 213), or use ground hazelnuts or unblanched almonds
50 g (2 oz) light Muscovado sugar

For serving
45 ml (3 tablespoons) blanched almonds, toasted

Whip together the yoghurt and cream and stir in the praline
or ground nuts. Divide between 4 small serving dishes, such
as ramekin dishes. Sprinkle on the sugar, cover and leave in
the refrigerator overnight. Sprinkle with the almonds to
serve. The sugar will have filtered through to make toffee-
like ripples in the cream!
Serves 4

FLAVOURED YOGHURT

Yoghurt is very much part of our way of life for many of us –
whether it is home-made, from full-fat or skimmed milk, or
bought in the supermarket. Here are a few high-fibre ways
to serve it.

To each 600 ml (1 pint) plain yoghurt, add the appropriate
ingredients according to your choice:

Prune
200 ml (7 fl oz) prune purée
50 g (2 oz) stoned prunes, chopped
5 ml (1 teaspoon) grated orange rind

Apricot
250 ml (9 fl oz) apricot purée
50 g (2 oz) dried apricots, chopped
30 ml (2 tablespoons) blanched almonds, flaked

Raspberry
175 g (6 oz) raspberries, hulled
150 ml (¼ pint) raspberry purée
15 ml (1 tablespoon) clear honey

Hazelnut
100 g (4 oz) hazelnuts, chopped
30 ml (2 tablespoons) dark Muscovado sugar

Honey and muesli
75 ml (5 tablespoons) clear honey
90 ml (6 tablespoons) Muesli base (1) or (2) (page 61)
30 ml (2 tablespoons) brazil nuts, chopped

CARDINAL CREAMS

Creamy rice and tangy raspberries make a good combination; experiment with other fruits, too.

25 g (1 oz) butter
600 ml (1 pint) milk
50 g (2 oz) brown rice, washed and drained
a pinch of grated nutmeg
30 ml (2 tablespoons) honey
150 ml (¼ pint) double cream, whipped
225 g (8 oz) raspberries, hulled

Melt the butter in a pan, add the milk, rice, nutmeg and honey and stir over low heat. Bring slowly to the boil, partly cover the pan and simmer gently for 1 hour, stirring occasionally, until the rice is tender and the milk has been absorbed. Remove from the heat and allow to cool. Fold in most of the cream, reserving a little for decoration.

Make layers of rice and raspberries (reserving a few for decoration) in 4 individual glasses, finishing with a rice layer. Pipe the reserved cream on top and arrange the remaining raspberries. Serve chilled.

Serves 4

RICE CAKES

One of those economical dishes – it uses a little cooked rice and other store-cupboard ingredients.

    4 eggs
    60 ml (4 tablespoons) cooked brown rice
    75 g (3 oz) sultanas
    25 g (1 oz) chopped mixed candied peel
    30 ml (2 tablespoons) light Muscovado sugar
    1.5 ml (¼ teaspoon) mixed ground spice
    grated rind of 1 small orange
    about 30 ml (2 tablespoons) wholewheat semolina
    oil, for shallow frying

For serving
    1 orange, quartered

Beat the eggs and stir in the rice, sultanas, peel, sugar, spice and orange rind. Mix in the semolina, adding a little more if needed to make a thick dropping consistency.

Heat the oil in a pan and when it is hot, drop tablespoons of the mixture into the pan. Fry over moderately high heat for 3–4 minutes or until the 'cakes' are well browned on the underside. Flip them over and fry the other sides until they are evenly brown. Serve hot, with a segment of orange.
Serves 4

* These rice cakes are good made with dried apricots (soaked, drained and finely chopped) and served with Apricot sauce (pages 222–3).

RICE PUDDING PLUS

It's sweetened and speckled with dried fruits and is surprisingly party-ish.

H.F.V.C.–K

100 g (4 oz) dried apricots, soaked and drained
100 g (4 oz) dried peaches, soaked and drained
100 g (4 oz) brown rice, washed and drained
900 ml (1½ pints) milk
2 eggs, beaten
60 ml (4 tablespoons) double cream
a pinch of grated nutmeg

For serving
150 ml (¼ pint) soured cream, beaten
30 ml (2 tablespoons) Demerara sugar

Chop the apricots and peaches. Put the rice and milk in a pan; bring slowly to the boil, stirring once or twice. Cover and simmer very gently for 1 hour, or until the rice is tender and has absorbed the milk. Remove the pan from the heat and beat in the eggs and double cream.

In a well-greased 1.4-litre (2½-pint) baking dish, spread a layer of rice; cover with half the mixed fruit, then more rice, followed by the remaining fruit and a final layer of rice. Sprinkle with nutmeg and cover the dish with foil.

Bake in a pre-heated oven, 180°C (350°F), Gas 4, for 25 minutes. Spread with the soured cream, sprinkle with the sugar and serve at once.
Serves 6

ALMOND PUDDING

225 g (8 oz) dried apricots, soaked and drained
50 g (2 oz) Demerara sugar
100 g (4 oz) blanched almonds, flaked
75 g (3 oz) butter
75 g (3 oz) light Muscovado sugar
2.5 ml (½ teaspoon) almond essence
2 eggs, separated
100 g (4 oz) self-raising wholewheat flour

For the topping
25 g (1 oz) blanched almonds (whole)

Spread the fruit in a greased 1.1-litre (2-pint) baking dish and sprinkle it with the Demerara sugar and half the flaked almonds. Beat together the butter and Muscovado sugar until light and fluffy, stir in the almond essence and beat in the egg yolks. Fold in the flour and the remaining flaked almonds. Stiffly whisk the egg whites and fold them into the mixture. Spread this over the fruit, level the top and sprinkle with the whole almonds.

Bake in a pre-heated oven, 180°C (350°F), Gas 4, for 45–50 minutes, until the topping is firm and golden brown. Serve hot.
Serves 4

* Use other soaked fruits from a mixed bag, or separate types – peaches and pears are the most successful.

BERRY CRUMBLE

225 g (8 oz) raspberries, hulled
450 g (1 lb) gooseberries, topped and tailed
30 ml (2 tablespoons) orange juice
100 g (4 oz) Demerara sugar

For the topping
100 g (4 oz) wholewheat flour
100 g (4 oz) hard margarine
100 g (4 oz) rolled porage oats
5 ml (1 teaspoon) ground cinnamon
30 ml (2 tablespoons) blanched almonds, split
30 ml (2 tablespoons) sesame seeds

Put the fruit in a 1.1-litre (2-pint) pie dish and add the orange juice and 25 g (1 oz) of the sugar.

Put the flour in a bowl, rub in the margarine until it is

grainy, stir in the remaining sugar, the oats, cinnamon, almonds and sesame seeds. Sprinkle the crumble topping over the fruit.

Bake in a pre-heated oven, 190°C (375°F), Gas 5, for 35–40 minutes, or until the top is crisp and hard.

Serves 4–6

* That's just the beginning. Adapt the recipe for any selection of fresh or dried fruits you like. It's delicious with cooked dried apricots; blackberries and apples; damsons and cooked dried pears – you choose. Plan ahead, cook some extra dried fruit and have it ready.

BLACKBERRY AND APPLE CRUMBLE

900 g (2 lb) blackberries, hulled
2 medium cooking apples, peeled, cored and very thinly sliced
30 ml (2 tablespoons) lemon juice
50 g (2 oz) Demerara sugar
a pinch of grated nutmeg

For the topping
175 g (6 oz) wholewheat flour
5 ml (1 teaspoon) ground ginger
100 g (4 oz) butter
50 g (2 oz) light Muscovado sugar
50 g (2 oz) ground hazelnuts

Put the fruit into a 1.1-litre (2-pint) baking dish and sprinkle with the lemon juice, Demerara sugar and nutmeg.

Mix together the flour and ginger, rub in the butter and stir in the sugar and nuts. Sprinkle the topping over the fruit.

Bake in a pre-heated oven, 190°C (375°F), Gas 5, for 45 minutes. Serve hot; though it's delicious cold.

Serves 4–6

BLACKCURRANT PUDDING

450 g (1 lb) blackcurrants, stripped from stalks
45 ml (3 tablespoons) water
125 g (5 oz) light Muscovado sugar
2 medium cooking apples, peeled, cored and thinly sliced
100 g (4 oz) soft margarine
2 eggs
125 g (5 oz) wholewheat flour
5 ml (1 teaspoon) baking powder
5 ml (1 teaspoon) mixed ground spice

Put the blackcurrants into a pan with the water and 25 g (1 oz) of the sugar. Bring to the boil over low heat, stirring to dissolve the sugar. Pour the fruit into a 1.1-litre (2-pint) pie dish and arrange the apple slices on top.

Beat together the remaining sugar and the margarine and gradually beat in the eggs. Mix together the flour, baking powder and spice and add little by little to the egg mixture. Beat well, spoon on top of the fruit and spread to level.

Bake the pudding in a pre-heated oven, 180°C (350°F), Gas 4, for 45–50 minutes, or until the spongy topping is well risen and firm. Serve hot.
Serves 4

POSH BREAD AND BUTTER PUDDING
The kind you can serve to company!

4 thin slices wholewheat bread, crusts removed, cut from
   a large loaf
50 g (2 oz) butter, softened
50 g (2 oz) currants
100 g (4 oz) sultanas
100 g (4 oz) chopped walnuts
75 g (3 oz) light Muscovado sugar
450 ml (¾ pint) single cream
3 eggs
45 ml (3 tablespoons) brandy

Spread the bread slices on both sides with the butter. Grease a 1.1-litre (2-pint) pie dish. Make layers of the bread, sprinkling each layer with currants, sultanas, walnuts and using 50 g (2 oz) of the sugar. Beat together the cream, eggs and brandy, pour over the pudding and set aside to soak for 1 hour.

Bake the pudding in a pre-heated oven, 180°C (350°F), Gas 4, for 35 minutes. Sprinkle the top with the remaining sugar and return to the oven for 10 minutes. Serve hot.
Serves 4

HONEY AND APRICOT MOULDS

100 g (4 oz) dried apricots, chopped
100 g (4 oz) self-raising wholewheat flour
5 ml (1 teaspoon) baking powder
100 g (4 oz) Demerara sugar
50 g (2 oz) chopped walnuts
100 g (4 oz) soft margarine
2 large eggs
90 ml (6 tablespoons) clear honey
6 walnut halves

For the apricot sauce
100 g (4 oz) dried apricots, chopped
60 ml (4 tablespoons) water
300 ml (½ pint) sweet cider
5 ml (1 teaspoon) lemon juice

Mix together all the pudding ingredients except the honey and walnuts and beat well. Grease 6 individual pudding (dariole) moulds and put 15 ml (1 tablespoon) of honey into each. Divide the pudding mixture between the moulds and level the tops. Cover each one with a circle of greased foil, pleated to allow for rising. Stand the moulds in a baking dish containing 5 cm (2 in) of hot water.

Cook the moulds in a pre-heated oven, 190°C (375°F), Gas 5, for 50 minutes. Turn them out, top each one with a walnut half and serve hot, with the sauce.

To make the sauce, simmer together the apricots, water and cider for 30 minutes, then stir in the lemon juice. Liquidize in a blender and serve hot.

Serves 6

HAZELNUT HALVA

Serve this Middle-Eastern 'delight' as a sweetmeat after a meal.

100 g (4 oz) butter
225 g (8 oz) light Muscovado sugar
3 large eggs, beaten
175 ml (6 fl oz) milk
75 g (3 oz) wholewheat flour
10 ml (2 teaspoons) baking powder
350 g (12 oz) wholewheat semolina
175 g (6 oz) chopped hazelnuts
grated rind of ½ lemon

For the syrup
425 ml (¾ pint) water
1 stick cinnamon
45 ml (3 tablespoons) lemon juice
a strip of lemon peel
350 g (12 oz) honey

Beat together the butter and sugar and gradually beat in first the egg mixture, a little at a time, and then the milk.

Mix together the flour and baking powder, then stir in the semolina, nuts and lemon rind. Gradually fold the dry ingredients into the egg mixture. Spread into a well-greased baking tin 23 × 18 cm (9 × 7 in) and level the top.

Bake the halva in a pre-heated oven, 180°C (350°F), Gas 4, for 45 minutes.

Meanwhile make the syrup. Put the ingredients into a pan, bring to the boil and simmer for 5 minutes, stirring to dissolve the honey. Remove from the heat and discard the cinnamon and the peel.

Pour the syrup evenly over the halva as soon as you take it from the oven. Leave until quite cold, then cut into small squares to serve.

PLUM DOWDY

A traditional country pudding with a crispy bread casing.

6 thin slices day-old wholewheat bread, cut from a large loaf
75 g (3 oz) butter
750 g (1½ lb) plums, halved and stoned
50 g (2 oz) blanched almonds
30 ml (2 tablespoons) clear honey
15 ml (1 tablespoon) water
45 ml (3 tablespoons) Demerara sugar
2.5 ml (½ teaspoon) ground ginger

Spread the bread on one side with the butter. Line a well-greased 1.1-litre (2-pint) baking dish with the bread, buttered side up, cut to fit. Fill with the plums and almonds; melt the honey in the water and pour over the fruit. Cover with the remaining bread slices, buttered side up, and sprinkle with the sugar and ginger.

Bake in a pre-heated oven, 190°C (375°F), Gas 5, for 1-1¼ hours, or until the topping is crisp and deep golden brown. Serve hot.

Serves 4-6

MARZIPAN APPLES WITH MINCEMEAT SAUCE

4 large cooking apples, cored
50 g (2 oz) marzipan
25 g (1 oz) butter, flaked

For the sauce
100 g (4 oz) mincemeat (page 231)
30 ml (2 tablespoons) honey
30 ml (2 tablespoons) rum
15 ml (1 tablespoon) lemon juice

Make a shallow slit all around each apple to stop them from bursting. Arrange them in a well-greased shallow baking dish and fill the cores with the marzipan. Dot with the butter. Bake in a pre-heated oven, 180°C (350°F), Gas 4, for 45 minutes, or until the apples are just tender.

To make the sauce, put all the ingredients into a pan and bring just to the boil. Serve the apples and sauce piping hot, with plain yoghurt.
Serves 4

HONEY-BAKED BANANAS

8 small bananas
100 g (4 oz) seedless raisins
25 g (1 oz) butter, flaked
60 ml (4 tablespoons) clear honey
45 ml (3 tablespoons) rum
30 ml (2 tablespoons) lemon juice
100 g (4 oz) blanched almonds

Split each banana lengthways without cutting it right through. Pack the raisins in a line along the slits and close up the bananas. Arrange the fruit in a shallow, greased baking dish and scatter the pieces of butter over it.

Mix together the honey, rum and lemon juice, pour over

the fruit and sprinkle with the almonds. Cover the dish with foil.

Bake in a pre-heated oven, 180°C (350°F), Gas 4, for 15 minutes. Remove the foil, baste the bananas with the sauce and bake uncovered for a further 5 minutes. Serve hot. *Serves 4*

BANANA PANPERDY

A lightly spiced sweet omelette with a wickedly sticky fruit filling that children love.

   50 g (2 oz) butter
   2 12-mm (½-in)-thick slices wholewheat bread, cut from a
      large loaf
   30 ml (2 tablespoons) Demerara sugar
   2.5 ml (½ teaspoon) ground cinnamon
   50 g (2 oz) dried stoned dates, chopped
   50 g (2 oz) chopped walnuts
   30 ml (2 tablespoons) honey
   3 large eggs
   15 ml (1 tablespoon) light Muscovado sugar
   15 ml (1 tablespoon) water
   1 banana, thinly sliced

   For serving
   soured cream

Melt half the butter in a pan. Remove the crusts from the bread and cut it into cubes. Fry the bread in the butter, stirring to brown it evenly, until it is crisp and dry. Toss the croûtons at once in the Demerara sugar mixed with the cinnamon and set them aside.

Put the dates, walnuts and honey in a pan and heat slowly, until the honey has melted.

To make the omelette, beat together the eggs, Muscovado

sugar and water. Melt the remaining butter in an omelette pan and when it is hot, pour in the egg mixture and tip the pan to spread it evenly. Cook over a moderate heat until the omelette is lightly set.

Sprinkle most of the croûtons over one side of the omelette, cover with the sliced banana and then with the date mixture. Slide the omelette on to a heated plate, folding it in two. Sprinkle with the remaining croûtons and serve at once. Serve with soured cream.
Serves 2

* For a puffy soufflé omelette, separate the eggs. Beat the yolks with the sugar and water; stiffly whisk the whites and fold them in.

CHESTNUT GÂTEAU

You can make this dessert extra scrummy (if you're not dieting) by serving it with a chocolate sauce.

    450 g (1 lb) chestnuts
    75 g (3 oz) butter
    125 g (5 oz) light Muscovado sugar
    175 g (7 oz) plain chocolate, melted and cooled
    3 eggs
    100 g (4 oz) 81 per cent self-raising flour
    15 ml (1 tablespoon) rum
    150 ml (¼ pint) soured cream

Prick the chestnuts, cover them with water and boil for 30 minutes. Drain, peel off the skins and rub off the brown inner skins. Liquidize in a blender.

Cream together the butter and sugar until light and fluffy then beat in 100 g (4 oz) of the melted chocolate. Gradually beat in the eggs and flour alternately. Stir in 100 g (4 oz) of the chestnut purée and the rum. Pour the mixture into a greased 10-cm (8-in) sandwich tin lined with non-stick silicone paper.

Bake in a pre-heated oven, 190°C (375°F), Gas 5, for 35–40 minutes, or until the cake is firm. Cool a little in the tin then turn on to a wire rack to cool completely. Split the cake horizontally.

Beat the remaining chestnut purée and chocolate with the soured cream. Spread half over one layer, sandwich with the other and spread the top with the remaining chocolate filling.

Serves 8

HAZELNUT MERINGUE TORTE

4 egg whites
225 g (8 oz) light Muscovado sugar
100 g (4 oz) ground hazelnuts
5 ml (1 teaspoon) lemon juice

For the filling
150 ml (¼ pint) soured cream
150 ml (¼ pint) double cream
450 g (1 lb) dessert blackberries, hulled

Whisk the egg whites until they are very stiff. Add half the sugar and whisk until the mixture is stiff again. Mix together the nuts and the remaining sugar and fold into the mixture. Lightly stir in the lemon juice. Spread the mixture into two 22.5-cm (9-in) circles placed on baking trays previously greased and lined with non-stick silicone paper. Smooth the tops.

Bake in a pre-heated oven, 180°C (350°F), Gas 4, for 30 minutes. Remove from the oven, invert the meringue layers, peel off the paper and return to the oven, upside-down, for a further 5 minutes to dry the undersides. Leave to cool.

Beat the creams together and spread half on one meringue layer. Top with most of the berries and cover with the second meringue. Pipe cream rosettes on top of the torte and decorate with the reserved berries.

Serves 8

* Use other soft fruits instead – raspberries, loganberries or currants are all good.

* Or spread the first meringue layer with thick apricot purée, then with the cream. Decorate the top with blanched almonds.

* Or spread with filling made by beating 2 mashed bananas, 60 ml (4 tablespoons) desiccated coconut and 30 ml (2 tablespoons) rum into the whipped creams.

CHOCOLATE PUDDING

175 g (6 oz) 81 per cent self-raising flour
10 ml (2 teaspoons) cocoa or carob powder
2.5 ml (½ teaspoon) baking powder
75 g (3 oz) wholewheat breadcrumbs
100 g (4 oz) hard margarine, grated
100 g (4 oz) Demerara sugar
100 g (4 oz) small chocolate drops
50 g (2 oz) blanched walnuts, chopped
2 eggs, beaten
150 ml (¼ pint) milk

Mix together the flour, cocoa powder and baking powder. Stir in the breadcrumbs, margarine, sugar, chocolate drops and walnuts. Beat in the eggs and milk. Turn the mixture into a well-greased 1.1-litre (2-pint) pudding basin. Cover the top with greased foil, pleated to allow for rising. Stand on a trivet or folded cloth in a pan half-filled with boiling water. Bring quickly back to the boil, cover the pan and simmer for 1½ hours, topping up with more boiling water as needed.

Turn out the pudding and serve hot.

Serves 4-6

CHRISTMAS PUDDING

We have a great tradition of fibre-full puddings. Here is the most celebrated one of all! This recipe makes three, so keep on celebrating!

    550 g (1¼ lb) sultanas
    550 g (1¼ lb) seedless raisins
    400 g (14 oz) currants
    100 g (4 oz) chopped mixed candied peel
    100 g (4 oz) blanched almonds, chopped
    100 g (4 oz) chopped walnuts
    100 g (4 oz) wholewheat breadcrumbs
    225 g (8 oz) wholewheat flour
    100 g (4 oz) dark Muscovado sugar
    5 ml (1 teaspoon) salt
    5 ml (1 teaspoon) ground cinnamon
    2.5 ml (½ teaspoon) grated nutmeg
    2.5 ml (½ teaspoon) ground allspice
    3 eggs, beaten
    300 ml (½ pint) milk
    125 ml (4 fl oz) brandy
    juice and grated rind of 1 lemon
    225 g (8 oz) soft margarine

Mix together all the dry ingredients, beat in the eggs, milk, brandy and lemon juice and rind and stir well. Beat in the margarine and, as the mixture gets stiff, get everyone to take a turn. Cover, leave overnight and stir vigorously again.

Spoon the mixture into three well-greased 1.1-litre (2-pint) pudding basins. Cover with greased foil pleated in a

line along the top to allow for rising. Lower the basins on to
trivets or folded cloths in large saucepans half-filled with
boiling water. Bring quickly to the boil again, cover and
cook for 6 hours, topping up the saucepans with boiling
water as needed. (Alternatively, use a pressure cooker and
cook each pudding at high pressure for $1\frac{3}{4}$ hours. Follow
the directions in the booklet relating to your appliance.)
Remove from the pans and leave to cool.

Replace the covers with fresh, greased foil, wrap each
pudding in a polythene bag and seal. Store in a cool, dry
place for up to one year.

To reheat, boil in the same way for $2\frac{1}{2}$ hours (or use a
pressure cooker, following the manufacturer's instructions).
Serve with rum or brandy butter and whipped cream.

Each pudding serves 8

MINCEMEAT

It's good to have a supply of mincemeat to use as flan
fillings with fresh fruits, fruit purée or baked toppings. This
one, far, far away from the original meat-content recipe, is
moistened with apple purée and flavoured with brandy.

225 g (8 oz) seedless raisins
100 g (4 oz) sultanas
100 g (4 oz) currants
50 g (2 oz) dried apricots, chopped
25 g (1 oz) crystallized ginger, chopped
50 g (2 oz) mixed chopped candied peel
45 ml (3 tablespoons) honey
60 ml (4 tablespoons) brandy
5 ml (1 teaspoon) ground cinnamon
2.5 ml ($\frac{1}{2}$ teaspoon) grated nutmeg
2.5 ml ($\frac{1}{2}$ teaspoon) salt
225 g (8 oz) thick apple purée (fresh, frozen or canned)
grated rind and juice of 1 lemon

Mix together the dried fruits and the peel. Put the honey, brandy, spices, salt, apple purée, lemon juice and lemon rind into a small pan over moderate heat and bring to the boil. Remove the pan from the heat, give the contents a good stir and pour over the fruits. Stir well and leave to cool. Pack the mincemeat into clean jars, cover with waxed paper circles and transparent paper covers or with plastic-lined screw-on lids, and label. Store in a dry, dark place for up to 3 weeks, or in the refrigerator for 4 weeks.
Makes two 450-g (1-lb) jars

* See page 119 for a mincemeat flan recipe.

STEAMED PLUM PUDDING

    100 g (4 oz) 81 per cent self-raising flour
    5 ml (1 teaspoon) baking powder
    5 ml (1 teaspoon) ground cinnamon
    100 g (4 oz) light Muscovado sugar
    50 g (2 oz) chopped walnuts
    100 g (4 oz) soft margarine
    2 eggs
    125 g (5 oz) prunes, stoned and chopped

    For serving
    30 ml (2 tablespoons) clear honey

Mix together the flour, baking powder and cinnamon, stir in the sugar and nuts, beat in the margarine and, gradually, the eggs. Stir in the chopped prunes.

Turn the mixture into a well-greased 850-ml (1½-pint) pudding basin, cover with a piece of greased foil pleated to allow for rising and place on a trivet or folded cloth in a pan half-filled with boiling water. Bring the water quickly back to the boil, cover the pan and boil for 1½ hours, topping up with boiling water as needed.

Turn out the pudding and dribble the honey over the top. Serve hot, with single or soured cream.
Serves 4-6

* For two delicious alternatives, substitute chopped dried figs or stoned dates for the prunes.

11 Baking

Home baking seems the most natural, wholesome and delicious part of a vegetarian way of life – and it is. Using wholewheat flour, you considerably increase your daily fibre intake and add more nutrients, too. Slices of fresh bread with cheese and fruit; warm cheese baps with a bowl of vegetable soup; nut cookies to pack in a lunchbox; frosted carrot cake to serve with coffee or as dessert – all through the day the whole family can revel in the pure goodness of these high-fibre foods.

Look closely at many of these baking recipes and you will see that they are packed with valuable protein too – nuts and seeds in bread, teabread, cakes and biscuits; bread and teabread, gingerbread and even sandwich cake spread with cream cheese; warm wholewheat scones moist and tangy with grated cheese – all can play a significant part in balancing a healthy diet.

WHOLEWHEAT BREAD

The standard way to make your own delicious good honest bread!

1.4 kg (3 lb) wholewheat flour
15 ml (1 tablespoon) salt
25 g (1 oz) fresh yeast, or 15 g (½ oz) dried yeast

15 ml (1 tablespoon) dark Muscovado sugar
about 1 litre (1¾ pints) tepid water
25 g (1 oz) margarine

Mix together the flour and water in a bowl and put in a
low oven to warm. Put the fresh yeast in a bowl with the
sugar and 45 ml (3 tablespoons) of the water and mix to a
smooth paste. (Follow the maker's instructions for dried
yeast.) Set aside in a warm place until the mixture becomes
frothy.

Rub the margarine into the flour. Make a well in the
centre, and pour in the yeast mixture; mix it in and
gradually stir in the remaining water to make a soft dough.
Knead the dough, dusting it with a little flour, until it is
smooth. (Of course, the dough hook of an electric mixer
makes short work of all this.)

Cover the dough with oiled polythene and leave it in a
warm place for about 30 minutes, or until it has doubled in
size. Knead it again for 1 minute and divide it into four
pieces. Place each piece in a greased 450-g (1-lb) loaf tin.
Cover the tins and leave in a warm place for 20 minutes, to
rise again.

Bake in a pre-heated oven, 230°C (450°F), Gas 8, for 30
minutes. Lower the heat to 190°C (375°F), Gas 5, and
continue baking for a further 15 minutes. Test the bread –
it should sound hollow when the base of the loaf is tapped.
Makes four 450-g (1-lb) loaves

* When time is short, you can divide up the dough as soon
as it is smooth, place it in tins (or on a baking tray), cover
and leave for 30 minutes to rise, then bake without further
kneading and rising. This gives a closer, firmer texture.
* For wholewheat rolls, shape the bread after the first
rising into rounds a little larger than a golf ball. Arrange
well apart on baking trays and leave to rise again. Bake in

a pre-heated oven, 230°C (450°F), Gas 8, for 15–20 minutes, until the rolls feel really light.
* For a 'crown' loaf, arrange 10–12 rolls side by side in a circle, one in the centre, the others around it. Leave to rise, and then bake as for an ordinary loaf. Break off a roll-sized piece to serve.

FAST-RISING BREAD

You can make 'ordinary' wholewheat bread after only one rising – but it gives a close, heavier texture. This way, you save time but not lightness.

    1.4 kg (3 lb) wholewheat flour
    25 g (1 oz) dried yeast
    1 50-mg tablet Vitamin C
    15 ml (1 tablespoon) dark Muscovado sugar
    25 g (1 oz) margarine
    15 ml (1 tablespoon) salt
    about 850 ml (1½ pints) tepid water

Mix together in a bowl the yeast, vitamin tablet, 5 ml (1 teaspoon) of the sugar and 300 ml (½ pint) warm water and leave in a warm place for 15 minutes, to become frothy.

Reserve a little of the flour for dusting. Mix the remainder with the rest of the sugar, the margarine, salt and water. Pour on the yeast mixture and stir to form a dough. Turn on to a floured board, sprinkle with flour and knead until smooth and elastic. Divide into four equal pieces.

To make tin loaves, flatten each piece of dough to a rectangle the size of the top of a 450-g (1-lb) loaf tin, fold it over twice and place in the well-greased tin. Cover with greased polythene and leave to rise in a warm place for 30 minutes.

Bake in a pre-heated oven, 230°C (450°F), Gas 8, for

30–35 minutes, or until the loaves sound hollow when tapped underneath. Cool on a wire rack.
Makes four 450-g (1-lb) loaves

BRAN-PLUS BREAD

225 g (8 oz) wholewheat flour
225 g (8 oz) strong bread flour
45 ml (3 tablespoons) bran
2.5 ml (½ teaspoon) salt
15 ml (1 tablespoon) baking powder
50 g (2 oz) margarine
300 ml (½ pint) milk, plus a little for brushing
45 ml (3 tablespoons) rolled porage oats

Mix together the flours, bran, salt and baking powder and rub in the margarine. Stir in the milk and mix to a soft dough. Knead on a lightly-floured board until smooth. Shape into a round on a baking sheet, mark into quarters and brush the top with milk. Sprinkle thickly with the oats.

Bake in a pre-heated oven, 200°C (400°F), Gas 6, for 45 minutes, or until the loaf sounds hollow when tapped. Cool on a wire rack.
Makes one 20-cm (8-in) round loaf

RYE SEEDBREAD

350 g (12 oz) rye flour
20 ml (4 teaspoons) caraway seeds
2.5 ml (½ teaspoon) salt
5 ml (1 teaspoon) baking powder
50 g (2 oz) margarine
150 ml (¼ pint) plain yoghurt
150 ml (¼ pint) milk
1 egg

Mix together the flour, 15 ml (1 tablespoon) of the seeds, the salt and baking powder and rub in the margarine. Beat together the yoghurt, milk and egg, pour on to the dry ingredients and mix until smooth. Knead lightly on a floured board. Divide the mixture in half and shape each piece into a round ball. Brush the tops with milk and sprinkle with the remaining caraway seeds.

Bake in a pre-heated oven, 200°C (400°F), Gas 6, for 1 hour, or until the base of each loaf sounds hollow when tapped. Cool on a wire rack.

Makes two 15-cm (6-inch) loaves

IRISH SODA BREAD

450 g (1 lb) wholewheat flour
5 ml (1 teaspoon) salt
5 ml (1 teaspoon) bicarbonate of soda
10 ml (2 teaspoons) cream of tartar
25 g (1 oz) margarine
300 ml (½ pint) milk

Sift together the flour, salt, soda and cream of tartar and tip in the bran from the sieve. Rub in the margarine and mix in the milk to make a soft dough. Knead until smooth and shape into a 20-cm (8-in) round. Place on a floured baking sheet, score the top with diagonal lines. Prick all over with a fork.

Bake in a pre-heated oven, 220°C (425°F), Gas 7, for about 30 minutes, or until the bread is well risen and firm. Serve warm, and preferably on the day it is made.

Makes one 450-g (1-lb) loaf

* For herb bread, stir 10 ml (2 teaspoons) dried herbs into the dry ingredients. Oregano, marjoram and thyme are all good.

* For cheese bread, stir in up to 75 g (3 oz) grated Cheddar cheese and use a little less milk.

* For peanut or walnut bread, stir 50 g (2 oz) chopped nuts into the dry ingredients. You can substitute peanut butter for the margarine.

NEW ENGLAND SODA BREAD

An old American recipe for bread that is steamed, like a pudding, and is moist, crusty and delicious. Start the preparations the day before cooking.

    100 g (4 oz) wholewheat breadcrumbs
    100 g (4 oz) molasses
    100 g (4 oz) wholewheat flour
    100 g (4 oz) rye flour
    100 g (4 oz) corn meal
    10 ml (2 teaspoons) bicarbonate of soda
    5 ml (1 teaspoon) salt
    125 ml (4 fl oz) water

Soak the breadcrumbs in water overnight. Turn them into a sieve, press out any excess moisture, then press the crumbs through the sieve into a bowl. Stir in the molasses.

Sift together the flours, corn meal, soda and salt and tip in the bran from the sieve. Pour in the water and the molasses mixture and stir well.

Turn the mixture into two greased 600-ml (1-pint) ovenproof bowls or pudding basins, cover with greased foil and tie. Place on a trivet in large pans of boiling water, cover and steam for $3\frac{1}{2}$ hours. Top up with boiling water as necessary, so that it is constantly half-way up the bowls.

Remove the foil and stand the bowls on a board in the oven. Bake at 170°C (325°F), Gas 3, for 15 minutes to dry

the crusts. Stand the bowls on a wire rack to cool slightly before turning out. Serve warm or cold.
Makes two 450-g (1-lb) loaves

APRICOT SCONE ROUND

225 g (8 oz) wholewheat flour
5 ml (1 teaspoon) bicarbonate of soda
5 ml (1 teaspoon) mixed ground spice
2.5 ml (½ teaspoon) ground cinnamon
2.5 ml (½ teaspoon) salt
50 g (2 oz) margarine
100 g (4 oz) dried apricots, chopped
150 ml (¼ pint) yoghurt
milk, for brushing
30 ml (2 tablespoons) Demerara sugar

Sift together the flour, soda, spices and salt and tip in the bran. Rub in the margarine, stir in the apricots and mix in the yoghurt. Knead to a smooth dough and shape into a 23-cm (9-in) round. Place on a greased and floured baking sheet, brush the top with milk and sprinkle with the sugar. Mark into 8 wedges.

Bake in a pre-heated oven, 220°C (425°F), Gas 7, for 25 minutes. Cool on a wire rack. It's best served warm.
Makes 8 slices

* Use chopped dates in place of the apricots – just as good.

CHEESE BAPS

450 g (1 lb) wholewheat flour
5 ml (1 teaspoon) salt
10 ml (2 teaspoons) bicarbonate of soda
2.5 ml (½ teaspoon) mustard powder

1.5 ml (¼ teaspoon) cayenne pepper
75 g (3oz) margarine
175 g (6 oz) Cheddar cheese, grated
300 ml (½ pint) milk, plus a little for brushing
10 ml (2 teaspoons) lemon juice
30 ml (2 tablespoons) sunflower seeds

Sift together the flour, salt, soda, mustard and pepper and tip in the bran from the sieve. Rub in the margarine and stir in the cheese. Mix together the milk and lemon juice and stir into the dry ingredients. Knead to a smooth dough.

Divide the dough into 8 pieces and shape into rounds. Flatten them on a greased and floured baking sheet to a thickness of 2.5 cm (1 in). Brush with milk and sprinkle with sunflower seeds.

Bake in a pre-heated oven, 200°C (400°F), Gas 6, for 25 minutes. Cool on a wire rack. Super with soup!
Makes 8 baps

WATERCRESS SCONES

These scones must be quite the nicest accompaniment to soup. They're good with cheese and salad, too.

225 g (8 oz) wholewheat flour
20 ml (4 teaspoons) baking powder
2.5 ml (½ teaspoon) salt
50 g (2 oz) butter
100 g (4 oz) Cheddar cheese, grated
1 bunch watercress sprigs, chopped
70 ml (5 tablespoons) soured cream
milk, for brushing

Sift together the flour, baking powder and salt and tip in the bran from the sieve. Rub in the butter to make a crumb

H.F.V.C.-L

consistency, then stir in 75 g (3 oz) of the cheese, the watercress and the soured cream to make a soft dough.

Roll out the dough on a lightly-floured board to 2.5 cm (1 in) thick. Cut out rounds with a 5-cm (2-in) cutter.

Arrange the rounds on a floured baking sheet, brush the tops with milk and sprinkle with the remaining cheese. Bake in a pre-heated oven, 220°C (425°F), Gas 7, for 15–20 minutes, or until the scones are well risen and golden brown. Serve warm, if possible.

Makes 10–12 scones

MALT LOAF

   100 g (4 oz) seedless raisins
   50 g (2 oz) light Muscovado sugar
   100 g (4 oz) bran cereal
   15 ml (1 tablespoon) malt extract
   300 ml (½ pint) milk
   100 g (4 oz) 81 per cent self-raising flour
   5 ml (1 teaspoon) mixed ground spice
   50 g (2 oz) chopped walnuts
   1 egg white, for brushing
   30 ml (2 tablespoons) Demerara sugar

Mix together the raisins, sugar, bran, malt and milk and allow to stand for 20 minutes.

Stir in the flour, spice and walnuts and mix thoroughly. Turn into a greased 850-ml (1½-pint) loaf tin lined with greased greaseproof paper, brush the top with egg white and sprinkle on the sugar.

Bake in a pre-heated oven, 180°C (350°F), Gas 4, for 1 hour, or until the loaf is well risen and firm. Cool on a wire rack.

Makes one 750-g (1½-lb) loaf

BANANA TEABREAD

50 g (2 oz) margarine
45 ml (3 tablespoons) clear honey
275 g (10 oz) 81 per cent self-raising flour
7.5 ml (1½ teaspoons) baking powder
2.5 ml (½ teaspoon) salt
50 g (2 oz) light Muscovado sugar
2 bananas, mashed
100 g (4 oz) seedless raisins
50 g (2 oz) chopped walnuts
1 egg
150 ml (¼ pint) plain yoghurt, buttermilk or soured milk

Melt the margarine and honey in a pan. Mix together the flour, baking powder and salt and stir in the sugar, bananas, raisins and walnuts. Beat together the egg and yoghurt (or buttermilk or soured milk) and stir into the dry ingredients. Stir in the honey mixture and beat until smooth and glossy.

Pour the mixture into a greased 450-g (1-lb) loaf tin. Bake in a pre-heated oven, 180°C (350°F), Gas 4, for 1 hour, or until well risen and golden brown. Cool and store for 2–3 days before eating, sliced, with butter.
Makes one 450-g (1-lb) loaf

ORANGE SANDWICH CAKE

100 g (4 oz) soft margarine
100 g (4 oz) light Muscovado sugar
2 eggs, lightly beaten
100 g (4 oz) 81 per cent self-raising flour
5 ml (1 teaspoon) baking powder
15 ml (1 tablespoon) grated orange rind
45 ml (3 tablespoons) orange juice
50 g (2 oz) chopped walnuts

For the filling
100 g (4 oz) apricot jam
100 g (4 oz) cream cheese

For dusting
caster or icing sugar

Cream together the margarine and sugar and beat in the eggs. Sift together the flour and baking powder, tip in any bran and gradually stir these ingredients into the egg mixture. Beat in the orange rind, orange juice and the chopped walnuts. Divide the mixture between two greased and floured 18-cm (7-in) sandwich tins.

Bake in a pre-heated oven, 180°C (350°F), Gas 4, for 25 minutes, or until the cakes are firm but springy to touch. Cool slightly in the tins, then turn on to a wire rack to cool completely.

Spread one layer with jam, the other with cream cheese; sandwich the two layers together. Sift the sugar over the top to decorate.

Makes one 18-cm (7-in) cake

OLD ENGLISH ALE CAKE

225 g (8 oz) light Muscovado sugar
225 g (8 oz) margarine
2 eggs
350 g (12 oz) wholewheat flour
10 ml (2 teaspoons) baking powder
5 ml (1 teaspoon) mixed spice
a pinch of grated nutmeg
150 ml (¼ pint) brown ale
175 g (6 oz) sultanas
100 g (4 oz) seedless raisins
100 g (4 oz) currants

50 g (2 oz) dried stoned dates, chopped
50 g (2 oz) chopped walnuts
grated rind of 1 orange

Grease a 20-cm (8-in) cake tin and line the base and sides with greased greaseproof paper.

Cream together the sugar and margarine until light and fluffy. Gradually beat in the eggs, one at a time, alternating with a little flour to prevent the mixture from curdling.

Sift the remaining flour with the baking powder and spices and tip in the bran from the sieve. Gradually fold the flour into the egg mixture alternately with the ale, stirring between each addition. Stir in the dried fruits, walnuts and orange rind and turn the mixture into the prepared tin.

Bake in a pre-heated oven, 150°C (300°F), Gas 2, for 2-2¼ hours, or until a skewer pushed through the centre of the cake comes out clean. Stand the tin on a wire rack for at least 30 minutes before turning out the cake. When it is completely cold, wrap the cake in foil and store in an airtight tin for a few days before serving.
Serves 8–10

BARA BRITH

A traditional Welsh fruit bread, it is best served just warm, at teatime.

150 ml (¼ pint) warm milk
50 g (2 oz) light Muscovado sugar
15 g (½ oz) dried yeast
75 g (3 oz) margarine
450 g (1 lb) 85 per cent wheatmeal flour
5 ml (1 teaspoon) salt
5 ml (1 teaspoon) mixed spice
75 g (3 oz) currants

75 g (3 oz) seedless raisins
50 g (2 oz) chopped mixed candied peel
50 g (2 oz) chopped walnuts

Pour half the milk into a small bowl, stir in 5 ml (1 teaspoon) of the sugar and sprinkle on the yeast. Stir well and leave in a warm place for 10–15 minutes to become frothy.

Melt the margarine in the remaining milk. Mix together the flour and salt. Make a well in the centre and pour in the yeast liquid and the milk mixture. Mix well, cover and leave in a warm place to double in size. Meanwhile, mix together the remaining sugar, the spice, dried fruits, peel and nuts.

Knead the dough on a lightly-floured board. Push a dent in the centre, sprinkle on some of the fruit mixture and knead to blend it thoroughly. Continue adding fruit and kneading until all the fruit is well distributed. Press the dough into a greased and warmed 1-kg (2-lb) loaf tin. Cover loosely and leave in a warm place until the dough has risen above the top of the tin.

Bake in a pre-heated oven, 220°C (425°F), Gas 7, for 10 minutes. Reduce the heat to 200°C (400°F), Gas 6, and continue baking for 15–20 minutes, or until the loaf sounds hollow when tapped underneath. Cover the top of the loaf with foil for the last few minutes of cooking if it gets too brown.

Makes one 1-kg (2-lb) loaf

CARROT CAKE

The first time you offer this cake, it's probably as well to say it's a 'spiced cake'. Until they have tasted it, people are suspicious of the carrots!

175 g (6 oz) light Muscovado sugar
175 ml (6 fl oz) corn oil
3 eggs
5 ml (1 teaspoon) vanilla flavouring
100 g (4 oz) chopped walnuts
225 g (8 oz) carrots, grated
175 g (6 oz) wholewheat flour
50 g (2 oz) fine oatmeal
5 ml (1 teaspoon) baking powder
5 ml (1 teaspoon) bicarbonate of soda
5 ml (1 teaspoon) ground cinnamon
2.5 ml (½ teaspoon) ground ginger
5 ml (1 teaspoon) salt

For the frosting
175 g (6 oz) cream cheese
100 g (4 oz) icing sugar, sifted
2.5 ml (½ teaspoon) vanilla flavouring

For decoration
24 walnut halves

Beat together the sugar, oil, eggs and vanilla and stir in the chopped walnuts and carrots. Mix together the flour, oatmeal, baking powder, soda, spices and salt and gradually stir into the carrot mixture. Beat well. Grease a 22-cm (8½-in) cake tin and line it with greased greaseproof paper. Turn the mixture into the tin. Bake in a pre-heated oven, 180°C (350°F), Gas 4, for about 1 hour 10 minutes, or until the cake is firm but springy to the touch. Cool in the tin, then turn out on to a wire rack. Remove the paper and leave to cool completely.

Beat together the cream cheese, icing sugar and vanilla until smooth and spread over the cake's surface in peaks and down the sides of the cake. Arrange the walnut halves on the top.

Serves 12

WHEATMEAL GINGERBREAD

It's delicious spread with cottage or cream cheese.

225 g (8 oz) wholewheat flour
2.5 ml (½ teaspoon) salt
15 ml (1 tablespoon) ground ginger
2.5 ml (½ teaspoon) ground cinnamon
5 ml (1 teaspoon) bicarbonate of soda
40 g (1½ oz) dark Muscovado sugar
50 g (2 oz) dried stoned dates, chopped
50 g (2 oz) chopped mixed candied peel
50 g (2 oz) seedless raisins
100 g (4 oz) margarine
60 ml (4 tablespoons) black treacle
1 egg
150 ml (¼ pint) milk

Sift together the flour, salt, spices and soda and tip in the bran from the sieve. Stir in the sugar, dates, peel and raisins. Melt together the margarine and treacle and leave to cool. Beat together the egg and milk. Pour the syrup and milk mixtures into the dry ingredients and beat well.

Pour the gingerbread mixture into a lined and greased tin 23 × 18 cm (9 × 7 in). Bake in a pre-heated oven, 150°C (300°F), Gas 2, for 1 hour, or until the gingerbread is just firm. Stand the tin on a wire rack to cool. When the cake is quite cold, wrap in foil and store for a few days before serving.
Serves 8–12

APPLE AND CLOVE CAKE

225 g (8 oz) 81 per cent self-raising flour
a pinch of salt
2.5 ml (½ teaspoon) ground cloves

100 g (4 oz) margarine
100 g (4 oz) light Muscovado sugar
100 g (4 oz) seedless raisins
45 g (3 oz) walnuts, chopped
225 g (8 oz) cooking apples, peeled and cored and chopped
2 eggs, lightly beaten
1 large cooking apple, cored and thinly sliced
25 g (1 oz) Demerara sugar

Grease and line a 450-g (1-lb) loaf tin.

Sift together the flour, salt and cloves and tip in any bran from the sieve. Rub in the margarine until the mixture is like fine crumbs. Stir in the sugar, raisins, walnuts and chopped apples and beat in the eggs. Beat the mixture until smooth, then turn it into the prepared tin.

Bake in a pre-heated oven, 150°C (300°F), Gas 2, for 1¼ hours. Remove from the oven, arrange the apple slices down the centre of the loaf and sprinkle on the Demerara sugar. Continue baking for 30 minutes, or until a skewer pierced through the centre comes out clean. Serve warm or cold.

Makes one 450-g (1-lb) loaf

CHOCOLATE BRAN CAKE

50 g (2 oz) All-Bran cereal
225 ml (8 fl oz) milk
100 g (4 oz) margarine
100 g (4 oz) dark Muscovado sugar
2 eggs, beaten
100 g (4 oz) 81 per cent self-raising flour
75 g (3 oz) plain chocolate, melted

For the filling
150 g (5 oz) cream cheese

For the topping
50 g (2 oz) ground almonds, toasted
30 ml (2 tablespoons) blanched almonds, toasted

Grease two 18-cm (7-in) sandwich tins and line them with greased greaseproof paper. Put the cereal and milk into a small bowl and leave to soak for 10 minutes. Beat together the margarine and sugar then gradually beat in the eggs, sprinkling on a little flour if the mixture shows signs of curdling. Fold in the soaked bran and flour and stir in the cooled chocolate.

Turn the mixture into the prepared tins and bake in a pre-heated oven, 180°C (350°F), Gas 4, for about 25 minutes. Allow to cool slightly in the tins, then turn out on to a wire rack to cool completely. Sandwich the two layers together with half the cream cheese and spread the remainder on top. Sprinkle the top with ground almonds and decorate with whole almonds.

Makes one 18-cm (7-in) cake

SPICED POTATO CAKE

100 g (4 oz) soft margarine
175 g (6 oz) light Muscovado sugar
100 g (4 oz) mashed potato, warm
50 g (2 oz) plain chocolate, melted
2 eggs, beaten
100 g (4 oz) wholewheat flour
5 ml (1 teaspoon) baking powder
2.5 ml (½ teaspoon) ground cinnamon
1.5 ml (¼ teaspoon) grated nutmeg
1.5 ml (¼ teaspoon) ground cloves

a pinch of salt
40 g (1½ oz) bran
75 ml (5 tablespoons) milk
50 g (2 oz) blanched almonds, chopped

Cream together the margarine, sugar and potato and beat in the chocolate and eggs. Sift together the flour, baking powder, spices and salt and tip in the bran from the sieve and the extra bran. Stir into the chocolate mixture alternately with the milk. Stir in the almonds and beat until the mixture is smooth. Turn into a greased and floured 20-cm (8-in) square cake tin.

Bake in a pre-heated oven 190°C (375°F), Gas 5, for 45–55 minutes, or until a skewer pierced through the centre of the cake comes out clean. Turn out on to a wire rack to cool.

Makes one 20-cm (8-in) cake

GINGER ROCK CAKES

225 g (8 oz) 81 per cent self-raising flour
a pinch of salt
5 ml (1 teaspoon) ground ginger
100 g (4 oz) margarine
75 ml (3 oz) Demerara sugar
50 g (2 oz) sultanas
50 g (2 oz) dried stoned dates, chopped
1 egg, lightly beaten
about 15 ml (1 tablespoon) milk, to mix

Sift together the flour, salt and ginger and tip in any bran from the sieve. Rub in the margarine until the mixture is like crumbs. Stir in the sugar, sultanas and dates. Beat egg and milk into the dry ingredients. Use a little more milk, if necessary, to make a stiff dough.

Place heaped teaspoons of the mixture well apart on a greased baking sheet. Bake in a pre-heated oven 200°C (400°F), Gas 6, for 15 minutes, until the cakes are well risen and firm. Cool on a wire rack.

Makes about 12 cakes

BREAD PUDDING

   225 g (8 oz) stale wholewheat bread, without crusts
   125 g (5 oz) mixed dried fruits, e.g. currants, seedless
       raisins, sultanas
   50 g (2 oz) prunes, stoned and chopped
   5 ml (1 teaspoon) mixed ground spice
   2 eggs, beaten
   a little milk, to mix
   Demerara sugar, for dusting

Break up the bread, cover it with water and soak for 30 minutes. Drain the bread, squeeze it dry and break it into crumbs – or press through a coarse sieve. Mix with the dried fruits and spices, beat in the eggs and just enough milk to make a thick paste.

Turn into a greased baking tin and cook in a pre-heated oven, 180°C (350°F), Gas 4, for 1 hour. Sprinkle with the sugar, cut in squares and serve warm or cold.

Serves 8

WHOLEFOOD SHORTBREAD

   100 g (4 oz) wholewheat flour
   50 g (2 oz) rice flour, or wholewheat semolina
   50 g (2 oz) Demerara sugar
   100 g (4 oz) butter

Mix together the flour, rice flour (or semolina) and sugar, rub in the butter and pat the dough into a ball. Press into a greased 18-cm (7-in) sandwich tin and smooth the top. Prick all over with a fork and mark into 8 slices.

Bake in a pre-heated oven, 150°C (300°F), Gas 2, for 40–45 minutes, or until the edges turn golden brown. Cut into slices. When quite cold, store in an airtight tin.
Makes 8 slices

OATMEAL BISCUITS

100 g (4 oz) medium oatmeal
225 g (8 oz) wholewheat flour
salt
125 g (5 oz) margarine
50 g (2 oz) light Muscovado sugar
1 egg
60 ml (4 tablespoons) water

Mix together the oatmeal, flour and salt, rub in the margarine and stir in the sugar. Beat the egg together with the water and stir into the mixture to make a firm dough.

Knead the dough lightly and roll out on a lightly-floured board to 6 mm (¼ in) thick. Cut into rounds with a 5-cm (2-in) cutter, place on floured baking sheets and prick all over with a fork.

Bake in a pre-heated oven, 180°C (350°F), Gas 4, for 20 minutes. Cool on a wire rack and store in an airtight container.
Makes about 24 biscuits

PEANUT BISCUITS

125 g (5 oz) smooth peanut butter
75 g (3 oz) soft margarine
175 g (6 oz) light Muscovado sugar
1 egg
2.5 ml (½ teaspoon) vanilla essence
125 g (5 oz) wholewheat flour
2.5 ml (½ teaspoon) salt
2.5 ml (½ teaspoon) bicarbonate of soda
75 g (3 oz) raw peanuts, ground

Cream together the peanut butter, margarine and sugar until the mixture is light, then beat in the egg and vanilla. Sift together the flour, salt and soda and tip in the bran from the sieve. Gradually beat the dry mixture into the peanut butter mixture, then beat until smooth.

Shape the paste into 2.5-cm (1-in) balls, place them on a floured baking sheet and flatten with a knife. Sprinkle with the ground peanuts.

Bake the biscuits in a pre-heated oven, 190°C (375°F), Gas 5, for 10 minutes. Leave to cool, then transfer to a wire rack. When cold, store in an airtight container.
Makes about 42 biscuits

CURRANT FLAPJACKS

75 ml (3 tablespoons) molasses
75 g (3 oz) margarine
100 g (4 oz) light Muscovado sugar
150 g (5 oz) rolled porage oats
50 g (2 oz) currants

Measure the molasses into a pan (this is easier to do if you first heat the spoon so that the treacly substance will slide off it), add the margarine and sugar. Place the pan over low heat until the contents have melted. Stir in the rolled oats. Spoon the mixture into a greased 20-cm (8-in) round flan tin.

Bake in a pre-heated oven, 180°C (350°F), Gas 4, for 20 minutes. With a sharp knife, mark 8 wedge-shaped slices. Leave the flapjacks to harden and cool in the tin, then cut through the slices. Store in an airtight tin.

Makes 8 slices

OATY COCONUT BARS

45 ml (3 tablespoons) clear honey
100 g (4 oz) margarine
75 g (3 oz) light Muscovado sugar
75 g (3 oz) desiccated coconut
75 g (3 oz) rolled porage oats
50 g (2 oz) rye flakes

For the icing
175 g (6 oz) icing sugar, sifted
15 ml (1 tablespoon) lemon juice

Melt 30 ml (2 tablespoons) of the honey with the margarine. Mix together the sugar, coconut, oats and rye flakes and stir in the honey mixture. Spread into a greased Swiss-roll tin and bake in a pre-heated oven, 170°C (325°F), Gas 3, for 25 minutes. Leave to cool in the tin.

Mix the icing sugar and lemon juice with the remaining honey and blend to a smooth paste. Spread over the coconut mixture when it is completely cold. Cut into bars. Store in an airtight container.

Makes 20 bars

CHOCOLATE MUESLI FINGERS

Comes into the 'child's play' category. Popular with them, too!

50 g (2 oz) butter
60 ml (4 tablespoons) thick honey
275 g (10 oz) Muesli base (1) or (2) (page 61)

For the topping
175 g (6 oz) plain chocolate

Melt together the butter and honey and stir in the muesli. Spread into a lined and greased Swiss-roll tin and level into the corners. Bake in a pre-heated oven, 180°C (350°F), Gas 4, for 25–30 minutes.

Melt the chocolate in a bowl over a pan of hot water, beat it smooth and spread evenly over the cooled biscuit base. Leave to set, then mark into fingers. Cut through when the biscuit is completely cold. Store in an airtight container.

Makes 10–12 fingers

COCONUT COOKIES

100 g (4 oz) margarine
100 g (4 oz) light Muscovado sugar
1 egg
100 g (4 oz) 81 per cent self-raising flour
salt
a pinch of ground mace
100 g (4 oz) desiccated coconut
about 20 almonds, blanched

Beat together the margarine, sugar and egg. Mix together the flour, salt, mace and 75 g (3 oz) of the coconut and beat into the egg mixture.

Place 20 × 5 ml (1 teaspoon) of the mixture well apart on greased baking trays and sprinkle with the remaining coconut. Press an almond into each one.

Bake in a pre-heated oven, 180°C (350°F), Gas 4, for 20–25 minutes. Cool on a wire rack and when completely cold store in an airtight container.

Makes about 20 cookies

GINGER COOKIES

  50 g (2 oz) golden syrup
  50 g (2 oz) unsalted butter
  25 g (1 oz) light Muscovado sugar
  2.5 ml (½ teaspoon) bicarbonate of soda
  50 g (2 oz) wholewheat flour
  50 g (2 oz) rolled porage oats
  5 ml (1 teaspoon) ground ginger
  40 g (1½ oz) preserved ginger, drained and finely chopped

Melt together the syrup, butter and sugar, stir in the remaining ingredients and cool slightly. Shape into 20 walnut-sized balls and place well apart on greased baking sheets. Flatten each with a fork.

Bake in a pre-heated oven, 160°C (325°F), Gas 3, for 15 minutes, or until golden brown. Cool a little, then transfer to a wire rack. When cold, store in an airtight container.

Makes about 20 cookies

MACAROON COOKIES

  50 g (2 oz) ground almonds
  50 g (2 oz) caster sugar
  15 ml (1 tablespoon) ground rice

15 ml (1 tablespoon) thick honey
2 drops almond flavouring
1 egg white
about 12 almonds, blanched

Beat together all the ingredients except the whole almonds. Line a baking sheet with a piece of edible rice paper (or use non-stick silicone paper). Drop 12 × 5 ml (1 teaspoon) of the mixture, well apart, on to the baking sheet and press an almond into the top of each one. Bake in a pre-heated oven, 160°C (325°F), Gas 3, for 15–20 minutes, or until golden brown. Cool on a wire rack, then peel the cookies from the paper. The edible rice paper will adhere to the cookies; the silicone paper should be discarded.

Makes about 12 cookies

SESAME COOKIES

100 g (4 oz) wholewheat flour
2.5 ml (½ teaspoon) bicarbonate of soda
100 g (4 oz) sesame seeds
100 g (4 oz) margarine
100 g (4 oz) light Muscovado sugar
30 ml (2 tablespoons) thick honey
1 egg, beaten

Sift together the flour and soda, tip in the bran from the sieve and stir in the seeds. Beat together the margarine and sugar, then beat in the honey. Add the dry ingredients alternately with the egg and, when all is added, beat well.

Shape the mixture into a cylinder about 4 cm (1½ in) thick, wrap in film or foil and chill for at least 2 hours.

Cut the dough into 6-mm (¼-in) slices and place well apart on a greased baking sheet. Bake in a pre-heated oven,

180°C (350°F), Gas 4, for 15 minutes, or until golden brown. Cool on a wire rack and then store in an airtight container.

Makes about 36 cookies

There are a few basic sauces that crop up now and again throughout the book, grouped together here for quick reference. They are not intended in themselves to be the ultimate in fibre intake – more for flavour.

SWEET AND SOUR SAUCE

25 g (1 oz) margarine
1 medium onion, peeled and chopped
1 green pepper, seeded and chopped
2 stalks celery, thinly sliced
100 g (4 oz) dried apricots, soaked, cooked and drained
50 g (2 oz) sultanas
30 ml (2 tablespoons) honey
2.5 ml (½ teaspoon) ground allspice
15 ml (1 tablespoon) red wine vinegar
450 ml (¾ pint) vegetable stock (page 12)
salt and pepper
15 ml (1 tablespoon) cornflour
30 ml (2 tablespoons) orange juice

Melt the margarine in a pan and fry the onion, pepper and celery over moderate heat for 3–4 minutes, stirring once or twice. Purée with the apricots in a blender. Return the mixture to the pan with the sultanas, honey, spice, vinegar

and stock, season with salt and pepper and bring to the boil. Simmer for 10 minutes. Stir the cornflour into the orange juice, pour into the sauce and bring to the boil, stirring. Taste and adjust the seasoning if needed. Remove from the heat as soon as the sauce clears and thickens.
Makes about 600 ml (1 pint)

TOMATO SAUCE

Good with filled vegetables and pasta especially.

  25 g (1 oz) butter
  30 ml (2 tablespoons) olive oil
  1 small onion, peeled and finely chopped
  2 cloves garlic, peeled and crushed
  900 g (2 lb) tomatoes, skinned and chopped
  10 ml (2 teaspoons) dried basil, or 15 ml (1 tablespoon)
    fresh basil, if available
  15 ml (1 tablespoon) chopped fresh parsley
  5 ml (1 teaspoon) light Muscovado sugar
  30 ml (2 tablespoons) bran
  salt and pepper

Melt the butter and oil in a pan and fry the onion and garlic over moderate heat for 4 minutes, stirring once or twice. Add all the other ingredients, bring to the boil, cover and simmer for 45 minutes. Taste and adjust the seasoning if needed.

For a smooth sauce, liquidize in a blender.
Makes about 450 ml (³/₄ pint)

* Use canned tomatoes when fresh ones are not available.
* Add a chopped green or red pepper with the frying vegetables for a slightly more perky flavour.

MUSHROOM SAUCE

Another one that's good with filled vegetables and pasta.

    25 g (1 oz) butter
    1 small onion, peeled and finely chopped
    350 g (12 oz) mushrooms, sliced
    150 ml (¼ pint) vegetable stock (page 12)
    150 ml (¼ pint) double cream
    salt and pepper
    15 ml (1 tablespoon) chopped fresh parsley

Melt the butter in a pan and fry the onion over moderate heat for 4 minutes, stirring once or twice. Add the mushrooms, and allow to sweat over low heat, stirring often, for 5 minutes. Add the vegetable stock, increase the heat and simmer for 5 minutes until the liquid has almost evaporated. Stir in the cream, season with salt and pepper and stir in the parsley.
Makes about 300 ml (½ pint)

* Try soured cream and a couple of drops of lemon juice instead of the double cream. I prefer it.

LEMON SAUCE

Good with brassicas – broccoli and cauliflower especially.

    15 g (½ oz) butter
    15 g (½ oz) wholewheat flour
    300 ml (½ pint) vegetable stock (page 12)
    a pinch of nutmeg
    45 ml (3 tablespoons) double cream
    grated rind and juice of 1 small lemon
    salt and pepper

Melt the butter in a pan, stir in the flour and when it forms a roux pour on the stock, stirring. Bring to the boil and simmer for 5 minutes. Stir in the nutmeg, cream, lemon rind and juice and season with salt and pepper. Serve hot.
Makes about 300 ml (½ pint)

CURRY SAUCE

Makes bland vegetables like courgettes and marrow very special.

30 ml (2 tablespoons) oil
1 small onion, peeled and finely chopped
1 clove garlic, peeled and crushed
15 ml (1 tablespoon) Madras curry powder
10 ml (2 teaspoons) fennel seeds, crushed
150 ml (¼ pint) water
15 ml (1 tablespoon) bran
10 ml (2 teaspoons) tomato purée
10 ml (2 teaspoons) lemon juice
30 ml (2 tablespoons) mango or peach chutney, chopped
salt
150 ml (¼ pint) double cream
45 ml (3 tablespoons) blanched almonds, flaked

Heat the oil in a pan and fry the onion and garlic over moderate heat for 3 minutes, stirring once or twice. Stir in the curry powder and fennel seeds and cook for 1 minute. Add the water gradually, then the bran, tomato purée, lemon juice and chutney. Simmer for 5 minutes. Season with salt and stir in the cream and almonds. After that, just heat through.
Makes about 300 ml (½ pint)

FLAVOURED BUTTERS

It's very useful to have a small selection of flavoured butter in the freezer or refrigerator to glaze steamed or boiled vegetables, to sauté mushrooms (which were *made* for garlic butter), or to provide a shiny last-minute garnish to dishes. There's just one basic method, but countless different flavours. Here are a few.

Herb Butter
    100 g (4 oz) unsalted butter at room temperature
    30–45 ml (2–3 tablespoons) chopped fresh herbs – parsley, mint, marjoram, thyme, chervil, chives, or a mixture
    2–3 drops lemon juice
    pepper

Beat all ingredients together until smooth. Shape into a roll and close-wrap in film to store.
Makes about 100 g (4 oz)

Garlic Butter
    100 g (4 oz) unsalted butter at room temperature
    2 large cloves garlic, peeled and crushed
    2 spring onions (or 1 shallot), peeled and very finely chopped
    30 ml (2 tablespoons) chopped fresh parsley
    pepper

Beat all ingredients together until smooth. Close-wrap in foil to store.
Makes about 100 g (4 oz)

Orange Cashew Butter

> 100 g (4 oz) unsalted butter at room temperature
> 20 ml (4 teaspoons) grated orange rind
> 50 g (2 oz) cashew nuts, finely chopped or ground
> pepper

Beat all ingredients together until smooth. Close-wrap in foil to store.

Makes about 100 g (4 oz)

DATE CHUTNEY

An instant success with all spiced dishes.

> 225 g (8 oz) stoned dried dates, finely chopped
> 5 ml (1 teaspoon) ground turmeric
> 5 ml (1 teaspoon) garam masala
> 5 ml (1 teaspoon) salt
> 2 green chillies, seeded and finely chopped
> 30 ml (2 tablespoons) lemon juice
> 15 ml (1 tablespoon) chopped fresh coriander leaves (or use mint)

Beat all ingredients together to form a thick paste. Cover container and store in the refrigerator.

Makes about 225 g (8 oz)

Dietary Fibre Chart

This chart will help you form a clear idea of the foods that are highest in dietary fibre. From the sections listing Grains and Cereal Products (which of course include bread, pasta and pastry); Vegetables; Fruit; and Nuts, you can plan the dishes and whole menus that will give you a satisfactory daily fibre intake. A calorie count in the second column will also help you to use the recipes as an aid to slimming or maintaining a healthy weight.

The dietary fibre content of foods is expressed in grams per 100 grams – which also gives you the percentage fibre content. The calories (kcal) are expressed per 100 grams of each ingredient.

GRAINS AND CEREAL PRODUCTS

Food	Dietary fibre grams per 100 g	Calories (kcal) per 100 g
BARLEY, pearl, boiled	2.2	120
BRAN, wheat	44.0	206
CORNFLOUR	–	354
FLOUR		
wholewheat (100%)	9.6	318
brown (85%)	7.5	327

GRAINS AND CEREAL PRODUCTS (cont)

Food	Dietary fibre grams per 100 g	Calories (kcal) per 100 g
FLOUR (cont)		
white (72%)		
breadmaking	3.0	337
household plain	3.4	350
household self-raising	3.7	339
PASTA		
refined, boiled	—	117
wholewheat, boiled	10.0	327
OATMEAL, raw – coarse, medium and fine	7.0	401
RICE		
polished, boiled	0.8	123
brown, boiled	1.6	144
SOYA flour, full fat	11.9	447
BREAD		
wholewheat	8.5	216
Hovis wheatgerm	4.6	228
Hovis wholewheat	10.2	218
white	2.7	233
toasted	2.8	297
ROLLS, white starch-reduced	2.0	384
BREAKFAST CEREALS		
All-Bran	26.7	273
Cornflakes	11.0	368
Grapenuts	7.0	355
Bran buds	28.2	254
Bran flakes	11.8	315
Muesli (average)	7.4	368
Puffed Wheat	15.4	325
Ready Brek	7.6	390
Rice Krispies	4.5	372
Shredded Wheat	12.3	324
Special K	5.5	388
Sugar Puffs	6.1	348

GRAINS AND CEREAL PRODUCTS (cont)

Food	Dietary fibre grams per 100 g	Calories (kcal) per 100 g
BREAKFAST CEREAL (cont)		
Weetabix	12.7	340
BISCUITS		
Cream Crackers	3.0	440
Crispbread		
rye	11.7	321
wheat, starch-reduced	4.9	388
Digestive, plain	5.5	471
Matzo	3.9	384
Oatcakes	4.0	441
PASTRY, shortcrust		
white flour	2.8	593
wholewheat flour	7.6	560

VEGETABLES

Food	Dietary fibre grams per 100 g	Calories (kcal) per 100 g
ARTICHOKES		
globe, boiled	—	15
Jerusalem, boiled	—	18
ASPARAGUS TIPS, boiled	1.5	18
AUBERGINE, raw	2.5	14
BEANS		
French, boiled	3.2	7
runner, raw	2.9	26
boiled	3.4	19
broad, boiled	4.2	48

VEGETABLES (cont)

Food	Dietary fibre grams per 100 g	Calories (kcal) per 100 g
BEANS (cont)		
butter, boiled	5.1	95
haricot, boiled	7.4	93
BEANSPROUTS, canned	3.0	9
BEETROOT, raw	3.1	28
boiled	2.5	44
BROCCOLI TOPS, raw	3.6	23
boiled	4.1	18
BRUSSELS SPROUTS, raw	4.2	26
boiled	2.9	18
CABBAGE		
red, raw	3.4	20
Savoy, raw	2.5	26
boiled	2.5	9
spring, boiled	2.2	7
white, raw	2.7	22
winter, raw	3.4	22
boiled	2.8	15
CARROTS, raw	2.9	23
boiled	3.1	19
canned	3.7	19
CAULIFLOWER, raw	2.1	13
boiled	1.8	9
CELERIAC, boiled	4.9	14
CELERY, raw	1.8	8
boiled	2.2	5
CHICORY, raw	—	9
CUCUMBER, raw	0.4	10
ENDIVE, raw	2.2	11
HORSERADISH, raw	8.3	59
LEEKS, raw	3.1	31
boiled	3.9	24
LENTILS, split, boiled	3.7	99

VEGETABLES (cont)

Food	Dietary fibre grams per 100 g	Calories (kcal) per 100 g
LETTUCE, raw	1.5	12
MARROW, boiled	0.6	7
MUSHROOMS, raw	2.5	13
fried	4.0	210
MUSTARD AND CRESS	3.7	10
OKRA, raw	3.2	17
ONIONS, raw	1.3	23
spring, raw	3.1	35
PARSLEY	9.1	21
PARSNIPS, raw	4.0	49
boiled	2.5	56
PEAS		
fresh, boiled	5.2	52
frozen, boiled	12.0	41
canned, garden	6.3	47
processed	7.9	80
dried, boiled	4.8	103
split, boiled	5.1	118
chick, cooked	6.0	144
PEPPERS, green, raw	0.9	15
POTATOES		
old, boiled, flesh only	1.0	80
baked, in skins	2.5	105
old, chips, frozen	1.9	109
new, boiled, flesh only	2.0	76
canned	2.5	53
instant powder made-up	3.6	70
crisps	11.9	533
PUMPKIN, raw	0.5	15
RADISHES, raw	1.0	15
SALSIFY, boiled	—	18
SEAKALE, boiled	1.2	8

VEGETABLES (cont)

Food	Dietary fibre grams per 100 g	Calories (kcal) per 100 g
SPINACH, boiled	6.3	30
SPRING GREENS, boiled	3.8	10
SWEDES, boiled	2.8	18
SWEETCORN, boiled	4.7	123
canned kernels	5.7	76
SWEET POTATOES, boiled	2.3	85
TOMATOES, raw	1.5	14
TURNIPS, boiled	2.2	14
TURNIP TOPS, boiled	3.9	11
WATERCRESS, raw	3.3	14

FRUIT

Food	Dietary fibre grams per 100 g	Calories (kcal) per 100 g
APPLES		
eating, flesh only	2.0	46
cooking, raw, flesh only	2.4	37
stewed, peeled and cored	2.1	32
APRICOTS		
fresh, raw, no stones	2.1	28
stewed, no stones	1.7	23
dried, raw	24.0	182
stewed	8.9	66
canned	1.3	106
AVOCADO PEARS	2.0	223
BANANAS, raw, flesh only	3.4	79
BILBERRIES, raw	—	56

FRUIT (cont)

Food	Dietary fibre grams per 100 g	Calories (kcal) per 100 g
BLACKBERRIES, raw	7.3	29
stewed	6.3	25
CHERRIES		
eating, raw, stoned	1.7	47
cooking, raw, stoned	1.7	46
stewed, stoned	1.4	39
CRANBERRIES, raw	4.2	15
CURRANTS		
black, raw	8.7	28
stewed	7.4	24
red, raw	8.2	21
stewed	7.0	18
white, raw	6.8	26
stewed	5.8	22
dried	6.5	243
DAMSONS, raw, stoned	4.1	38
stewed, stoned	3.5	32
DATES, dried, stoned	8.7	248
FIGS		
green, raw	2.5	41
dried, raw	18.5	213
stewed	10.3	118
GOOSEBERRIES		
green, raw	3.2	17
stewed	2.7	14
ripe, raw	3.5	37
GRAPES		
black, raw, flesh only	0.4	61
white, raw, flesh only	0.9	63
GRAPEFRUIT, raw, flesh only	0.6	22
canned	0.4	60

FRUIT (cont)

Food	Dietary fibre grams per 100 g	Calories (kcal) per 100 g
GREENGAGES, raw, stoned	2.6	47
stewed	2.2	40
GUAVAS, canned	3.6	60
LEMONS, whole	5.2	15
LOGANBERRIES, raw	6.2	17
stewed	5.7	16
canned	3.3	54
MEDLARS, raw	10.2	42
MELONS		
cantaloupe, flesh only	1.0	24
honeydew, flesh only	0.9	21
watermelon, flesh only	—	21
MULBERRIES, raw	1.7	36
NECTARINES, raw, stoned	2.4	50
OLIVES, stoned	4.4	103
ORANGES, flesh only	2.0	35
PASSION FRUIT, whole	6.7	34
PEACHES		
fresh, raw, stoned	1.4	37
dried, raw	14.3	212
stewed	5.3	79
canned	1.0	87
PEARS		
eating, whole	1.7	29
cooking, peeled, cored and stewed	2.5	30
canned	1.7	77
PINEAPPLE		
fresh, flesh only	1.2	46
canned	0.9	77
PLUMS		
Victoria dessert, raw, stoned	2.1	38

FRUIT (cont)

Food	Dietary fibre grams per 100 g	Calories (kcal) per 100 g
PLUMS (cont)		
cooking, raw, stoned	2.5	26
stoned and stewed	2.2	22
stewed without sugar	2.0	20
PRUNES		
dried, raw, stoned	16.1	161
stoned and stewed	8.1	82
QUINCES, raw, flesh only	6.4	25
RAISINS, dried, stoned	6.8	246
RASPBERRIES, raw	7.4	25
stewed	7.8	26
canned	5.0	87
RHUBARB, stewed	2.4	6
STRAWBERRIES, raw	2.2	26
canned	1.0	81
SULTANAS, dried	7.0	250
TANGERINES, raw, flesh only	1.9	34

NUTS

Food	Dietary fibre grams per 100 g	Calories (kcal) per 100 g
ALMONDS, shelled	14.3	565
BARCELONA NUTS, shelled	10.3	639
BRAZIL NUTS, shelled	9.0	619
CHESTNUTS, shelled	6.8	170
COB or HAZELNUTS, shelled	6.1	380
COCONUT, fresh, shelled	13.6	351
desiccated	23.5	604

NUTS (cont)

Food	Dietary fibre grams per 100 g	Calories (kcal) per 100 g
PEANUTS, fresh, shelled	8.1	570
roasted and salted	8.1	570
PEANUT BUTTER, smooth	7.6	623
WALNUTS, shelled	5.2	525

Index

COOKING FOR GOOD HEALTH BOOKS NOW AVAILABLE IN GRANADA PAPERBACKS

Susan Beedell
Pick, Cook and Brew   £1.50 ☐

Ursula Gruniger
Cooking with Fruit   50p ☐

Sheila Howarth
Grow, Freeze and Cook   £1.50 ☐

Kenneth Lo
Cooking and Eating the Chinese Way   £1.50 ☐
The Wok Cookbook   £1.25 ☐

L D Michaels
The Complete Book of Pressure Cooking   £1.25 ☐

Franny Singer
The Slow Crock Cookbook   £1.50 ☐

Janet Walker
Vegetarian Cookery   £1.50 ☐

Beryl Wood
Let's Preserve It   95p ☐

COOKERY HANDBOOKS NOW AVAILABLE IN GRANADA PAPERBACKS

L D Michaels
The Complete Book of Pressure Cooking   £1.95 ☐

F Marian McNeil
The Scots Kitchen   £1.95 ☐
The Scots Cellar   £1.95 ☐

Cecilia Norman
Pancakes & Pizzas   95p ☐
Micro-Wave Cookery Course   £1.50 ☐

David Scott
The Japanese Cookbook   £1.50 ☐

Franny Singer
The Slow Crock Cookbook   £1.50 ☐

E P Veerasawmy
Indian Cookery   £1.50 ☐

Janet Walker
Vegetarian Cookery   £1.50 ☐

Pamela Westland
Bean Feast   £1.50 ☐
The Everyday Gourmet   75p ☐
Food for Keeps   £1.95 ☐
The Complete Grill Cookbook   £1.50 ☐

Carol Wright
Complete Meat Cookery   £1.25 ☐

Arto Der Haroutunian
Complete Arab Cookery   £1.50 ☐

REGIONAL COOKERY BOOKS NOW AVAILABLE IN GRANADA PAPERBACKS

Jean M Graham
The Poldark Cookery Book   £1.50 ☐

Sheila Hutchins
Grannie's Kitchen
Recipes from the North of England   95p ☐
Recipes from East Anglia   95p ☐
Recipes from the West Country   £1.25 ☐

F Marian McNeil
The Scots Kitchen   £1.95 ☐
The Scots Cellar   £1.95 ☐

Marika Hanbury Tenison
West Country Cooking   £1.25 ☐

HB481

COOKERY HANDBOOKS NOW AVAILABLE IN GRANADA PAPERBACKS

Elizabeth Cass
Spanish Cooking · £1.25 □

Jean Graham
The Poldark Cookbook · £1.50 □

Ursula Gruniger
Cooking With Fruit · 50p □

Marika Hanbury Tenison
Deep-Freeze Cookery · £1.95 □
New Fish Cookery · £1.25 □
West Country Cooking · £1.25 □
The Best of British Cooking · £1.50 □
Cooking with Vegetables · £1.95 □

Sheila Howarth
Grow, Freeze and Cook · £1.50 □

Robin Howe
Greek Cooking · £1.25 □
German Cooking · £1.50 □

Sheila Hutchins
Grannie's Kitchen
Recipes from the North of England · 95p □
Recipes from East Anglia · 95p □
Recipes from the West Country · £1.25 □

Kenneth Lo
Cooking and Eating the Chinese Way · £1.50 □
The Wok Cookbook · £1.50 □

Jennifer Stone
The Alcoholic Cookbook · £1.25 □

Arto Der Haroutunian
Complete Arab Cookery · £1.50 □

HB581

All these books are available at your local bookshop or newsagent, and can be ordered direct from the publisher.

To order direct from the publisher just tick the titles you want and fill in the form below:

Name _____

Address _____

_____

Send to:
Granada Cash Sales
PO Box 11, Falmouth, Cornwall TR10 9EN

Please enclose remittance to the value of the cover price plus:

UK 45p for the first book, 20p for the second book plus 14p per copy for each additional book ordered to a maximum charge of £1.63.

BFPO and Eire 45p for the first book, 20p for the second book plus 14p per copy for the next 7 books, thereafter 8p per book.

Overseas 75p for the first book and 21p for each additional book.

Granada Publishing reserve the right to show new retail prices on covers, which may differ from those previously advertised in the text or elsewhere.